Emotional Indigestion Illness Shaping Bodies, Families, and Communities

Branny Mthelebofu

Published by Banny Joma Enterprise, 2025.

EMOTIONAL INDIGESTION ILLNESS SHAPING BODIES, FAMILIES, AND COMMUNITIES

First edition. September 20, 2025.

ISBN: 979-8232077679

Written by Branny Mthelebofu.

Also by Branny Mthelebofu

The Healing We Never Spoke Of: Therapy
Emotional Indigestion: Illness Shaping Bodies, Families, and Communities
Emotional Indigestion Illness Shaping Bodies, Families, and Communities
Research and Innovation: Strategies for Managers and Entrepreneurs

Watch for more at https://www.facebook.com/branny.smithsa/.

To the silent ones—who swallowed their pain because there was no room to speak.

To the healers—who carried others while their own wounds remained unseen.

To the daughters and sons—who inherited burdens that were never theirs to bear.

And to every community still learning thatwhat is repressed does not disappear,but waits to be transformed.

This book is for you.

Emotional Indigestion:

Illness Shaping Bodies, Families, and Communities

“What we repress returns—healing begins when silence is broken.”

Johannesburg
E-mail: brannysmithsa@gmail.com
South Africa
Johannesburg
Social Media: @ Branny Smith
@ Branny Mthelebofu

Printed in South Africa, Pretoria.

Banny Joma Enterprise publishers

About The Author

Dr Branny Mthelebofu is a South African clinical researcher, public health advocate, and published author with a strong academic foundation in medical microbiology, health systems research, and community-based interventions. He is a multi-talented filmmaker, Holistic Nutrition Practitioner, Holistic Counselor and a researcher who is spending his time writing or sharing ideas or teaching. He is a teacher and an instructor of communication strategy and research innovation. As a scriptwriter, he creates stories that will push you to think again about life and future choices. He has been teaching nutrition on radio for many years on a weekly basis sharing with listeners about the best ways to live a healthy lifestyle.

His peer-reviewed research includes studies on microbial profiles in diabetic foot ulcers and systemic delays in breast cancer diagnosis within South Africa's public health sector—both reflecting his commitment to improving outcomes in underrepresented and vulnerable populations.

In addition to his scientific contributions, Branny is a dynamic communicator and author under the pen name **Branny Smith**, producing accessible self-help and wellness literature. His work bridges biomedical science with narrative therapy, addressing mental health, behavior change, and community empowerment.

Dr Branny Mthelebofu brings a unique interdisciplinary perspective rooted in clinical experience, social justice, and culturally grounded care—making him a valuable voice in Indigenous health, LMIC-focused research, and global health delivery.

"I am especially drawn to your project's emphasis on health equity and Indigenous leadership in care delivery. As someone working in South Africa, a nation marked by profound inequities and a complex health history, I understand the importance of community-led innovation, culturally grounded research methods, and policy advocacy in achieving sustainable change. My skills in evidence-based public health, qualitative and

epidemiologic methods, and cross-sector collaboration would contribute meaningfully to your multidisciplinary team."

His works span both scientific publications and popular mental-health-oriented books, as well as film and therapeutic content aimed at character-driven storytelling and holistic well-being.

My recent publications in peer-reviewed journals—including studies on diabetic foot infections and oncology delays—reflect my commitment to addressing real-world disparities in access and outcomes.

Prologue

There are illnesses we can name, measure, and treat with precision. A broken bone shows clearly on an X-ray. High blood pressure can be tracked on a machine. Cancer can be located on a scan, and medication prescribed accordingly. These ailments command our attention because they are visible, diagnosable, and recognized by medical systems.

But there is another illness—less visible, yet no less deadly—that lives silently within families, communities, and even entire nations. It begins not in the body but in the soul. It is born of unspoken pain, of silenced grief, of unmet needs, of words swallowed rather than expressed. This is what I call emotional indigestion: the accumulation of unprocessed feelings that slowly, persistently, and often tragically, eat away at health, identity, and hope.

In every village, city, and household, people carry this silent weight. The woman who stays in a marriage she never chose, her own desires buried beneath duty and fear. The man who feels trapped by expectations of masculinity, unable to cry, unable to speak, slowly unraveling under the pressure. The elderly who numb themselves with alcohol, hoping to quiet memories of abandonment or regret. The young who reach for drugs, risky sex, or escape, misunderstood as reckless when, in fact, they are desperately trying to balance unbearable emotions.

What is striking is not just the existence of this hidden suffering, but how little it is understood or acknowledged—by professionals, by politicians, by families themselves. We treat strokes, yet overlook the decades of unprocessed anger that helped fuel them. We prescribe medication for hypertension, but rarely ask about the heartbreak, the betrayal, the loneliness that gave rise to it. We respond to suicides as individual tragedies without addressing the collective silence that makes life unbearable for so many.

This book is an invitation to break that silence. Drawing on psychoanalytic insights from Freud and Jung, interwoven with stories from rural villages and urban cities alike, it explores how emotions denied and repressed do not disappear—they return, often in the body, in our relationships, or in destructive behaviors.

I write this as both a therapist and a fellow human being who has seen how much people suffer in silence. Emotional indigestion is not a metaphor; it is a crisis that shapes families, reshapes communities, and quietly determines who thrives and who breaks.

And yet, there is hope. Healing begins the moment we dare to name what we feel, to honor the body's cry as the soul's hunger, and to reclaim our voices from the prisons of silence.

This book is my offering to that journey—toward awareness, toward healing, and toward the possibility of living as whole, unburdened selves.

I did not come to write this book out of theory alone, but out of the lived weight of what I call emotional indigestion. For years, I witnessed how unspoken pain coils itself quietly in the body, how unresolved grief reshapes families, and how silence can eat away at whole communities. I have seen strong men collapse under invisible burdens, women carry generations of unvoiced sorrow, and young people numb their raw wounds with substances, intimacy, or the reckless edge of death itself.

This book was born in the villages where people rarely say, I am hurting. It was born in the crowded clinics where physical pain is treated, but emotional wounds remain untouched. It was born in the quiet homes where women cannot leave abusive marriages because they have nowhere else to go. It was born in the voices of the elderly who turn to alcohol or pills because they cannot find words for their despair. And it was born in the eyes of young men and women whose lives end too soon, not because they wanted to die, but because they could not find another way to silence the storm inside.

Professionals call it trauma, depression, anxiety, or addiction. I call it emotional indigestion—the accumulation of unprocessed pain that the body and mind no longer know how to carry. It is what happens when emotions are swallowed but never digested, when society punishes vulnerability and rewards silence, when culture denies people the language to speak their truth. The body remembers what the mouth cannot say.

This is not only a personal problem. It is a global health crisis. Across the world, families are breaking down under the unseen weight of repressed emotions. Communities are eroded by stigma, violence, and neglect. Politicians and professionals continue to miss the connection between emotional suffering and the illnesses filling our hospitals. The cost is not only measured in suicide rates, substance abuse, or broken homes—it is measured in lost potential, fractured societies, and a humanity that is slowly forgetting how to heal itself.

In these pages, I invite you to journey with me through stories, reflections, and therapeutic insights. I draw from the wells of Freud and Jung, from community voices in rural villages and city streets, and from the quiet chambers of therapy rooms. My aim is not to pathologize human suffering, but to name it, to understand it, and to reclaim the possibility of healing.

If what we repress always returns, then our silence will keep haunting us. But if we dare to break the silence, if we dare to face what has been swallowed, then healing—personal and collective—becomes possible.

This is not only my story. It is yours, too. It is our story as families, communities, and a global society. And it begins here, with the courage to face our emotional indigestion. There are wounds that never bleed, yet they wound us all the same. There are cries that never escape the lips, yet they echo endlessly inside. There are stories buried so deeply in families and communities that they are never told—but their silence still shapes us.

This is what I call emotional indigestion. The unprocessed, unspoken pain that sits heavy inside, demanding to be noticed even when ignored. It is grief, shame, fear, and loneliness swallowed whole, only to return as illness of body, mind, and spirit.

We see its traces everywhere. In rural villages, where women live in marriages they did not choose, bound by duty but starved of self. In the cities, where professionals wear polished smiles while suffocating under invisible weights. Among the youth, whose confusion and despair turn to substances, violence, or escape. Even among the elderly, who, instead of being honored for wisdom, often numb themselves with alcohol or medication to quiet decades of unspoken sorrow.

Healthcare systems treat the consequences—high blood pressure, ulcers, anxiety, addiction—but rarely the root cause. Politicians debate social issues without naming the silence and repression beneath them. Communities see broken homes, suicides, and rising substance abuse, but few dare to ask: what is this pain we keep swallowing?

This book is my attempt to give it a name. To bring voice to what has been silenced, and light to what has been hidden. To show that emotional indigestion is not just a private struggle, but a public health crisis, a global wound.

Because what we repress will always return. Because no soul was meant to carry pain in silence. Because healing is possible—but only when we face what we have long denied.

There are wounds that never bleed. There are cries that never leave the mouth. There are stories that never reach the ears of the world.

I call this emotional indigestion. The pain we swallow but never digest. The sorrow we bury until it lives inside our bones.

It is the hidden illness shaping bodies, breaking families, haunting communities.

In the villages, it wears the face of women trapped in marriages they never chose. In the cities, it hides in the silence of professionals who smile while drowning. Among the youth, it burns as addiction, rebellion, despair. Even the elders—once pillars of wisdom—now turn to bottles or pills to numb their grief.

Hospitals see the strokes, the ulcers, the broken hearts. Society sees the suicides, the drugs, the shattered homes. But rarely do we see the root: the storm of emotions never given room to breathe.

This book is about breaking that silence. About naming what has long been unnamed. About daring to face what we have swallowed for generations.

Because healing begins the moment we stop hiding. Because what we repress always returns. Because the soul—heavy as it may be—was never meant to carry pain alone.

This book is born from a simple but haunting observation: people across the world—whether in a remote Limpopo village, in the bustling streets of Lagos, or the skyscrapers of New York—are swallowing their emotions whole. They do not digest their pain, grief, or unmet desires. Instead, they bury them. The result is what I call emotional indigestion.

Emotional indigestion is not a metaphor only; it is an embodied reality. Suppressed feelings return in the form of headaches, ulcers, hypertension, depression, and even intergenerational cycles of silence. Freud gave us the language of the unconscious: attachment, repression, transference, ego dissolution. Jung reminded us of archetypes and shadows, where what we deny becomes what we inherit. Across cultures, traditional healers, churches, and therapists have tried to soothe this condition—sometimes with wisdom, sometimes with avoidance. What struck me in my research and encounters is this: healing is both personal and collective. A woman in a rural village, silenced by patriarchy, holds the same indigestion as a man in London who hides his tears behind his professional success. A therapist guiding others through grief may be silently drowning in her own unprocessed sorrow. A pastor blessing marriages may himself be trapped in a union that suffocates him. Helpers, too, are not exempt. This book does not set out to criticize any one culture or tradition. Instead, it attempts to map how emotional pain becomes public health—how silence, stigma, and fear turn personal wounds into generational epidemics. Through stories, psychoanalytic reflection, and culturally grounded insights, it explores how emotional indigestion lives in our bodies, our families, and our communities. It is my conviction that healing requires courage: the courage to face the fear of starting over, the fear of losing status, the fear of being alone, and even the fear of going back to simplicity after attaining wealth. True therapy—whether through psychoanalysis, traditional rituals, church prayer, or holistic medicine—must lead us to face what we have swallowed but never digested. This book is not written only for academics or therapists, but for anyone who has ever felt the weight of an unspoken grief. It belongs to communities in pain. It belongs to women who inherited silence from their mothers. It belongs to men whose masculinity has been weaponized against their own vulnerability. And it belongs to the healers, pastors, therapists, and helpers who must also confront their own unresolved indigestions before they can walk with others toward healing. The journey is both deeply personal and unmistakably global. My hope is that these pages will act as a mirror, a companion, and perhaps, an invitation—to pause, to reflect, to speak, and to finally digest what has been buried for too long.

Foreword

This book is born from a simple but haunting observation: people across the world—whether in a remote Limpopo village, in the bustling streets of Lagos, or the skyscrapers of New York—are swallowing their emotions whole. They do not digest their pain, grief, or unmet desires. Instead, they bury them. The result is what I call emotional indigestion.

Emotional indigestion is not a metaphor only; it is an embodied reality. Suppressed feelings return in the form of headaches, ulcers, hypertension, depression, and even intergenerational cycles of silence. Freud gave us the language of the unconscious: attachment, repression, transference, ego dissolution. Jung reminded us of archetypes and shadows, where what we deny becomes what we inherit. Across cultures, traditional healers, churches, and therapists have tried to soothe this condition—sometimes with wisdom, sometimes with avoidance.

What struck me in my research and encounters is this: healing is both personal and collective. A woman in a rural village, silenced by patriarchy, holds the same indigestion as a man in London who hides his tears behind his professional success. A therapist guiding others through grief may be silently drowning in her own unprocessed sorrow. A pastor blessing marriages may himself be trapped in a union that suffocates him. Helpers, too, are not exempt.

This book does not set out to criticize any one culture or tradition. Instead, it attempts to map how emotional pain becomes public health—how silence, stigma, and fear turn personal wounds into generational epidemics. Through stories, psychoanalytic reflection, and culturally grounded insights, it explores how emotional indigestion lives in our bodies, our families, and our communities.

It is my conviction that healing requires courage: the courage to face the fear of starting over, the fear of losing status, the fear of being alone, and even the fear of going back to simplicity after attaining wealth. True therapy—whether through psychoanalysis, traditional rituals, church prayer, or holistic medicine—must lead us to face what we have swallowed but never digested.

This book is not written only for academics or therapists, but for anyone who has ever felt the weight of an unspoken grief. It belongs to communities in pain. It belongs to women who inherited silence from their mothers. It belongs to men whose masculinity has been weaponized against their own vulnerability. And it belongs to the healers, pastors, therapists, and helpers who must also confront their own unresolved indigestions before they can walk with others toward healing.

The journey is both deeply personal and unmistakably global. My hope is that these pages will act as a mirror, a companion, and perhaps, an invitation—to pause, to reflect, to speak, and to finally digest what has been buried for too long.

Epigraph

What is silenced in words is remembered in the body; what is denied in one soul returns in another. Healing begins when we dare to digest our pain. What we refuse to feel, the body will remember.

Drawn from Sigmund Freud and Carl Jung theories about healing.

Praise for Author

Dr Branny Mthelebofu is a rare voice who bridges science, storytelling, and community wisdom. His work carries both the rigor of research and the empathy of lived experience."

"As Branny Smith, he writes with clarity and compassion, transforming complex ideas into words that heal, inspire, and empower."

"His academic research into health disparities and clinical care in South Africa demonstrates a commitment not only to knowledge but also to justice. His publications bring critical visibility to issues often ignored."

"Whether through scientific articles, community health advocacy, or creative writing, Branny's words resonate with purpose. He has the gift of reaching both professional and everyday audiences with equal authenticity."

"Readers describe his work as thought-provoking and deeply human—an invitation to reflect, to question, and to act."

Creative writer, public health advocates and filmmaker with multiple talents.

If you want to engage in happiness, negotiations, problem solving, how to catch difficult people to understand your needs, then this writer is the one to be your friend, just catch up all the readings to understand this statement. - Filmmaker with purpose and a Holistic Nutrition Practitioner with a purpose. He has notice emotional indigestion when he was teaching Sunday school children and started to learn about crisis counselling. In that period, he was still a university student, but through spiritual counselling he has noticed that there is a form of pain through the children that manifest from their parents at home.

Acknowledgement

I acknowledge the life and my partner, her appreciation and sincerity is keeping me alive through spirituality and humanity. This book could not have been written without the many voices, stories, and silences that shaped its pages. I am indebted to the women and men in rural villages, urban centers, churches, and clinics who trusted me with their experiences of love, loss, repression, and resilience. Your courage in speaking—and sometimes in staying silent—revealed to me the depth of what I have come to call *emotional indigestion*.

I wish to thank colleagues in psychoanalysis, psychology, public health, and anthropology who continually reminded me that theory and practice must walk together. Your critiques, debates, and insights kept this work honest and expansive.

To the healers, therapists, and pastors who opened their doors and their lives: thank you for showing me that those who guide others are often carrying wounds of their own, and that true healing begins with acknowledging our shared vulnerability.

Special gratitude goes to my mentors, who pushed me to weave Freud's and Jung's insights into the fabric of today's global crises, and to my peers who reminded me that scholarship has a heartbeat—that ideas are only meaningful when they reach those who need them most.

To my family and friends: thank you for bearing with me through long hours of writing, re-writing, and wrestling with questions that do not always have easy answers. Your patience and encouragement grounded me when the work felt overwhelming.

Finally, I acknowledge the countless unnamed individuals around the world whose struggles with silence, dependency, and repression continue every day. This book is written for you, with the hope that naming what has been hidden might open a door to healing.

Epigraph

What is silenced in words is remembered in the body; what is denied in one soul returns in another. Healing begins when we dare to digest our pain.

What we refuse to feel, the body will remember. Drawn from Sigmund Freud and Carl Jung theories about healing.

Why does silence make us sick?

From women in rural villages to men in global cities, from pastors to therapists, people everywhere carry unspoken pain. This book calls it emotional indigestion—the grief, fears, and desires we swallow but never process.

Blending the insights of Sigmund Freud and Carl Jung with real stories from communities in Africa, Europe, America, and beyond, this book shows how unhealed emotions become illness, how trauma is passed down through generations, and why even healers themselves are not exempt.

But it is not only about analysis—it is about freedom. Each section closes with reflective tools to help you face hidden fears, break cycles of silence, and begin digesting what has long been buried.

More than a theory, this book is a companion for healing—an invitation to transform pain into strength and reclaim the fullness of life.

Emotional Indigestion: Psychoanalysis, Community, and Intergenerational Trauma

This book situates emotional suffering at the intersection of psychoanalysis, public health, and cultural practice. Drawing from Freud's concepts of repression, transference, and ego structures, alongside Jung's theories of the collective unconscious and archetypes, it frames emotional indigestion as both an intrapersonal conflict and a communal inheritance.

By weaving together narratives from diverse contexts—African villages, urban centers in Europe and the Americas, and the experiences of healers themselves—the book illustrates how unprocessed emotional material contributes to:

- The burden of psychosomatic illness in low-resource

communities

- Intergenerational patterns of dependency and silence
- The perpetuation of stigma around therapy and healing practices

For scholars, practitioners, and policy leaders, this text underscores the urgent need to integrate psychoanalytic understanding into public health discourse. It proposes that emotional digestion is not only a matter of individual therapy but also of community resilience, collective healing, and health system innovation.

1. Introduction

The Unseen Weight of the Soul- The Invisible Wound

Emotional indigestion is one of the most unacknowledged crises of our time. Unlike a broken bone, it leaves no immediate scar on an X-ray. Unlike a bleeding wound, it cannot be dressed with bandages. Instead, it hides in the inner corridors of the psyche, spilling out into the body, into behaviors, into addictions, and in too many tragic cases—into death by suicide.

Professionals often miss it because they are trained to categorize symptoms within narrow diagnostic frames: depression, anxiety disorder, hypertension, substance abuse.

Ordinary people miss it because cultural narratives teach them that emotions must be endured quietly, that life is hard and pain is "just part of being human." Politicians miss it because they are too invested in statistics and infrastructure to ask: what is the quality of our inner lives?

What does it mean that people across all social classes feel so alone that they would rather die than confess their despair?

The irony is that emotional indigestion is everywhere. It is in the ulcers of the farmer who never speaks his grief, in the hypertension of the widow who hides her longing for love, in the insomnia of the wealthy businessman who cannot let go of a hollow marriage. It is in the teenagers numbing themselves with nyaope, alcohol, or sex, not out of pleasure but out of desperation to silence a restlessness that words cannot carry. It is in the old man who drinks himself into forgetfulness because the memories of lost comrades, failed dreams, and wasted years have become too heavy to face.

Yet we call these things "individual weakness," "sin," "bad choices," or "lifestyle diseases." Rarely do we name them for what they are: the body crying out because the heart and mind have been silenced.

Why Professionals Misunderstand

In therapeutic rooms—even with the best intentions—professionals can miss emotional indigestion because their frameworks are overly compartmentalized. Medicine sees blood pressure, but not grief.

Psychiatry diagnoses depression, but misses the cultural weight of being a woman in a patriarchal village who cannot leave her marriage without social exile. Psychology, in its more Western forms, sometimes insists on "cognitive restructuring" when the wound is not in the thought but in the buried rage of being unseen for decades.

Freud taught that repression is the cornerstone of neurosis. What is unbearable to the ego is pushed into the unconscious, where it remains alive, active, and forceful. For many in South Africa—whether in Limpopo's villages or in Pretoria's suburbs—the unbearable is not one thing, but a lifetime of things: poverty, gender roles, unemployment, violence, betrayal, and silence. Each unspoken moment is swallowed.

Over time, the psyche becomes constipated with unresolved affect, and the body begins to ache under the weight.

Yet a clinician seeing a hypertensive patient rarely asks: What heartbreak have you been swallowing these last twenty years?

The professional world has split the body from the soul, treating them as separate domains. In doing so, the essence of emotional indigestion—its psychosomatic nature—is misunderstood.

Why Ordinary People Misunderstand

Ordinary people misunderstand emotional indigestion because they live inside cultural scripts that equate silence with strength. A woman in Bolobedu may be told, "Your tears dishonor your marriage." A man in Rustenburg may be mocked if he admits he feels useless without work. A young girl in Mpumalanga may be told that her sadness is simply "a spirit attack" rather than a reaction to years of emotional neglect.

Because pain has no safe space for expression, it is hidden beneath the surface.

Communities become experts at denial. People explain illness as bad luck, or witchcraft, or "too much thinking." In doing so, they keep the cycle alive. The wound is never named, so it festers.

Suicide becomes the final silence—an act of desperation when all other ways of balancing emotions fail. For the one who takes their life, it is not necessarily that they wished for death. It is that life, filled with swallowed grief, became impossible to digest.

Why Politicians Misunderstand

Politicians misunderstand emotional indigestion because their focus is on visible progress: roads, schools, hospitals, jobs. These are necessary, but they cannot replace the need for inner healing. The unspoken assumption is that once poverty is alleviated, people will simply "be well." Yet even among the wealthy, emotional indigestion thrives.

A politician's wife may suffer panic attacks every night, terrified that leaving an abusive marriage will ruin her social standing.

A successful businessman may drive a luxury car, but the emptiness in his heart leads him to alcohol, sex with strangers, and eventually depression.

Emotional indigestion does not disappear with money—it only changes its mask.

Thus, when suicide rates rise, politicians respond with platitudes: "We must fight depression." But they do not see that the depression is not only chemical—it is cultural, social, and deeply emotional. It is indigestion of decades of repression.

Suicide and the Crisis of Indigestion

Increasingly, people turn to suicide because they feel there is no other outlet for their pain. In Freud's language, the death drive—the unconscious pulls towards release from tension—becomes more powerful than the life instincts. When love, community, and meaning have been blocked, the psyche seeks release in annihilation.

In Limpopo villages, young men facing chronic unemployment use rope, poison, or the gun to end their lives. Their families say, "We never saw it coming," but the signs were there: silence, isolation, heavy drinking. In Sandton, young professionals jump from buildings, overdose, or crash their expensive cars, their deaths disguised as accidents. The common denominator is not poverty or wealth, but the impossibility of digesting life's unspoken wounds.

Substances, Sex, and the Search for Balance

When suicide is not chosen, people often turn to substitutes—substances or sexual intimacy—as attempts to balance emotional indigestion. The old man in a North West township drinks every night, not for pleasure but for anesthesia. He numbs the pain of memories never spoken. The grandmother in Limpopo takes painkillers more often than necessary, not for physical pain but for loneliness.

The youth, overwhelmed by unprocessed emotions, turn to drugs like nyaope, cannabis, or alcohol. These substances offer temporary relief, a simulated balance. Yet in reality, they deepen the indigestion, piling more repression on top of old wounds.

Sexual intimacy, too, becomes a misused medicine. Some chase endless affairs, confusing bodily release with emotional healing.

Others cling desperately to partners, hoping that physical closeness will soothe the emptiness inside. But without true emotional digestion, sex becomes another failed attempt at balance—momentary relief followed by deeper hunger.

The Youth and Misunderstanding

Young people today carry perhaps the heaviest weight of emotional indigestion. They inherit the unprocessed traumas of their parents—poverty, broken marriages, apartheid legacies, silences—and they also face their own crises of identity in a fast-changing world. They are told to "be strong" while battling mental storms that are never acknowledged.

When they turn to drugs, communities call them "useless." When they seek pleasure in sex, they are labeled immoral. When they withdraw, they are shamed as lazy.

Rarely does anyone ask: What pain is this child trying to silence? What wound is eating them from within?

Youth suicide is thus rising, not because young people are weak, but because society has made it impossible for them to name their emotional indigestion without stigma.

Towards Healing

To understand emotional indigestion is to see that healing cannot be limited to medicine or to preaching willpower. It requires spaces where people can safely name their pain without fear of shame, judgment, or exile. It requires professionals who see beyond diagnoses into the psychosomatic expressions of repression. It requires politicians who recognize that infrastructure alone cannot heal the human soul.

Most of all, it requires ordinary communities to unlearn silence—to allow men to cry, women to leave abusive marriages, youth to speak their despair without ridicule.

Healing begins when the repressed is allowed to surface, when the inner ache is named, digested, and transformed into meaning.

Until then, emotional indigestion will remain one of the most destructive silent epidemics of our time—an epidemic of swallowed grief, numbed bodies, and silenced souls.

Emotional Indigestion: Psychoanalysis, Public Health, and Communities in Pain

Human beings are relational creatures, yet across cultures, they carry within them wounds that they cannot fully name, process, or release. This book proposes the term emotional indigestion to describe the psychological, emotional, and physical consequences of unresolved grief, unspoken fears, and suppressed desires.

Emotional indigestion occurs when feelings and experiences are swallowed but never fully digested, accumulating instead in the psyche and body, shaping relationships, health outcomes, and intergenerational patterns of suffering.

Drawing on the foundational insights of Sigmund Freud and Carl Jung, this book situates emotional indigestion at the intersection of psychoanalysis, cultural practice, and public health. Freud's work on repression, transference, attachment, and ego dissolution illuminates how the unconscious exerts control over behaviors, thoughts, and emotions long after conscious intentions fail.

According to Freud, unresolved early attachments leave traces in the unconscious that later emerge in adult relational patterns, often as dependency, anxiety, or compulsive attachment. A child raised with inconsistent care may internalize insecurity, manifesting in adulthood as the inability to separate identity from a partner, leading to profound dependency syndrome.

Jung complements this analysis by expanding the frame to the collective unconscious and archetypes. He demonstrated that psychological suffering is not solely individual; entire communities inherit patterns of repression and trauma. Archetypal figures—the Wounded Healer, the Great Mother, the Absent or Authoritative Father—recur across cultures, influencing how sons, daughters, and broader social groups internalize and replicate dependency, silence, and unprocessed emotion. When unaddressed, these inherited patterns result in cycles of emotional indigestion across generations, appearing as psychosomatic illness, relational dysfunction, or social malaise.

In every culture, in every community, human beings carry wounds they cannot easily name.

Freud once described repression as the mind's way of keeping unacceptable desires and unbearable grief out of conscious awareness. Jung extended this, warning that what is banished from the personal mind does not disappear—it sinks into the collective unconscious, where it reemerges in dreams, symptoms, and patterns of fate. It is from these insights that we arrive at the language of emotional indigestion: the condition in which unprocessed experiences, swallowed but not integrated, accumulate in both the psyche and the body.

This book proposes that emotional indigestion is not simply a private psychological phenomenon. It is also a public health issue—a silent epidemic manifesting in psychosomatic illness, intergenerational trauma, and collective suffering within families, churches, and entire villages.

When communities are taught to repress—whether through silence, stigma, or rigid traditions—they do not digest the pain of betrayal, abandonment, or fear. Instead, this pain is metabolized into stress-related diseases, broken relationships, cycles of violence, and profound disconnection from self and others.

Freud's psychoanalysis helps us see how attachment, repression, and transference form the scaffolding of indigestion. A child raised with inconsistent care internalizes anxiety as an unconscious template for future relationships, forever fearing abandonment or rejection. Later, this unresolved dependency surfaces in adult attachments, where fear of being alone leads to clinging, silence, or staying in destructive unions.

Jung deepens this understanding by showing that communities themselves hold archetypal wounds: the "Wounded Healer" who guides others but cannot heal himself, the "Great Mother" who nurtures but also binds daughters into cycles of dependency, the "Father" who disciplines but withholds affection, leaving sons uncertain of their masculinity.

But psychoanalysis alone cannot capture the cultural realities in which indigestion is lived. In African villages, women who suffer physical illness are often told they are bewitched, when in fact their bodies are breaking under the weight of unspoken marital grief.

In European cities, professionals pride themselves on independence, but beneath their polished surfaces lie the same unprocessed losses—masked with alcohol, workaholism, or compulsive striving.

In churches from Nigeria to the United States, healing is sought through prayer alone, yet the congregation remains full of pastors and members alike who are silently choking on repressed desires and unresolved trauma.

The epidemiological lens further shows us how emotional suffering becomes measurable in terms of health outcomes. Stress is a determinant of disease, influencing rates of hypertension, stroke, and mental illness in vulnerable populations. Silence and stigma amplify this burden by preventing individuals from seeking timely care. Moreover, indigestion is not just intrapersonal but intergenerational: mothers model dependency for daughters, fathers model silence for sons, and communities inherit these patterns as unquestioned truths.

Yet, there is hope. Emotional indigestion, once named, can be digested. Psychoanalysis gives us a method: tracing the symptoms back to early experiences of loss, dependency, or abandonment, and bringing them into awareness where they can be transformed.

Jung reminds us that the unconscious is not only a site of repression but also a source of creativity, renewal, and archetypal strength. Traditional healing practices, when joined with therapeutic insight, can offer rituals of release that reconnect the body and spirit to the possibility of wholeness.

This book, therefore, is not only an academic study but also a call to courage. To face indigestion requires confronting fears of change, of poverty, of loneliness, and of losing status. It requires therapists, pastors, and healers to acknowledge their own unresolved pain before they can effectively help others. Most of all, it requires communities to move beyond silence—to speak, to listen, and to reimagine emotional suffering not as weakness, but as the very terrain through which true health and liberation are born.

We often think of illness as something that starts in the body — high blood pressure from too much salt, ulcers from poor diet, or fatigue from overwork. Yet beneath the surface of many conditions lies an unspoken truth: the body is carrying emotions that were never processed, never named, and never released. This is what I call emotional indigestion.

Just like the stomach struggles to break down food when it is overwhelmed, our minds and hearts can also fail to "digest" painful experiences.

Loss, humiliation, abandonment, fear, or betrayal — when such emotions are swallowed whole without expression or support, they do not disappear. Instead, they ferment inside us, becoming tension in the chest, migraines that return without warning, restless nights, or unexplained exhaustion.

Over time, this hidden indigestion corrodes both the mind and body.

The tragedy is that most people do not recognize this link. Doctors treat only the body, politicians speak only about economics, and families often dismiss emotional struggles with phrases like "be strong" or "you'll get over it." But silence has consequences. Across rural villages and bustling cities alike, people are drowning in unprocessed emotion. Some numb themselves with alcohol or drugs; others use sexual intimacy as a substitute for genuine emotional connection. The youth are misunderstood as "rebellious" or "lazy," when in reality many are simply trying to survive the unbearable weight of their feelings. Even elders, once considered resilient, increasingly lean on substances or isolation because they have no safe space to release their grief.

Emotional indigestion is not a weakness — it is a human response to a world that offers few avenues for healthy expression. What we need is a cultural shift: spaces where vulnerability is not shamed, where therapy is not a luxury, and where emotions are treated with the same seriousness as broken bones. Healing begins not with medication alone, but with learning how to name, feel, and digest our emotional lives before they consume us.

Case Examples Across Regions

The lived realities of emotional indigestion manifest in diverse settings. In rural villages of Zimbabwe and Swaziland, women frequently present with physical ailments such as hypertension, chronic fatigue, and ulcers. While these symptoms are often attributed to "witchcraft" or spiritual attack, in many cases they stem from prolonged emotional repression within unhealthy marital relationships.

Women, raised to believe they cannot survive without a man, endure dependency syndrome compounded by poverty, lack of education, and social expectation. They rarely seek therapy, and even when clinics exist, stigma and silence prevent disclosure. This illustrates Freud's insight into repression: the psyche suppresses unbearable realities, yet the body somatically carries the unresolved distress.

In urban environments such as New York, London, and Sydney, men and women in high-pressure professional contexts demonstrate a different but related pattern. Dependency may manifest less as poverty-driven survival and more as psychological attachment to status, wealth, or social recognition. Here, emotional indigestion shows itself in workaholism, chronic anxiety, insomnia, or cardiovascular strain. Even therapists and pastors are not exempt: a therapist may counsel clients to leave toxic relationships while remaining trapped in her own, illustrating

Jung's archetype of the Wounded Healer—those who guide others yet carry unprocessed pain themselves.

In West African nations such as Ghana and Nigeria, communities often rely on churches as both therapeutic and social institutions. Pastors provide guidance, counseling, and spiritual remedies, but these systems sometimes unintentionally perpetuate emotional indigestion.

Parishioners may be encouraged to remain in oppressive relationships for the sake of social respectability, reinforcing Freud's principle of repression and Jung's concept of collective unconscious: unspoken cultural norms solidify patterns of dependency and intergenerational suffering. Similarly, traditional healers may attempt holistic remedies without addressing the underlying unconscious trauma, leaving emotional indigestion unprocessed.

In European countries such as Greece and France, women and men face another form of emotional indigestion: the fear of losing status, lifestyle, or social recognition. Even when independent and financially secure, the fear of returning to a simpler life or confronting one's inner emptiness creates paralysis. Psychoanalytic interpretation explains that this fear is rooted in both early attachment patterns and culturally inherited archetypes: the shadow self, the ego's dissolution, and the internalized authority figures who conditioned dependence and shame.

Emotional Indigestion as a Public Health Problem

Beyond personal suffering, emotional indigestion has measurable epidemiological consequences. Stress is a well-established determinant of disease. In low-resource communities, chronic stress caused by unprocessed emotional pain contributes to hypertension, cardiovascular disease, and stroke.

In villages across Limpopo, Gabon, and Zimbabwe, patterns of relational stress correlate with increased prevalence of gastrointestinal and cardiovascular illnesses, illustrating the psychosomatic pathways Freud theorized. Globally, similar patterns are seen among professionals experiencing chronic workplace stress coupled with relational dependency, showing that emotional indigestion transcends socioeconomic boundaries.

Intergenerational transmission compounds the problem. Children observe and internalize parental patterns of dependency, repression, and silence. Girls are socialized to believe they cannot thrive without a partner, while boys learn to suppress vulnerability in the name of socially constructed masculinity. These lessons become unconscious templates that perpetuate emotional indigestion across generations, as Jung predicted in his work on archetypes and inherited psychic content.

The Role of Silence, Stigma, and Suppression

Silence, stigma, and cultural norms magnify emotional indigestion. Across continents—from African villages to Western metropolises—individuals refrain from speaking about relational pain, fearing social judgment, gossip, or shame.

Freud's theory of repression illuminates how unacknowledged emotions resurface as neuroses or somatic illness, while Jung reminds us that these suppressed collective patterns affect communities and families as much as individuals.

Consider a village in Gabon: multiple women fall ill, not due to spiritual attack, but because their relational pain is unspoken, untreated, and socially unacknowledged. Their mothers' lives modeled endurance of dependency and suppression, which children internalize unconsciously.

Over time, the village manifests collective symptoms: sickness, early death, and disrupted family structures. Emotional indigestion becomes a public health crisis, not just a private psychological concern.

Psychoanalytic Pathways to Healing

Healing emotional indigestion requires both courage and method. Freud's psychoanalysis offers a pathway: tracing symptoms to early attachment experiences, bringing unconscious patterns into consciousness, and working through repression. Jung complements this by showing that acknowledging and integrating archetypal shadows—the parts of self-denied or feared—transforms inherited patterns of suffering.

Traditional and communal forms of healing, such as ritual, prayer, or community storytelling, are effective when they address not only cultural or spiritual dimensions but also the psychological root of suffering. Churches and traditional healers can become sites of psychoanalytic intervention if they facilitate recognition and expression of previously repressed emotion.

The book also emphasizes that therapists, pastors, and healers must confront their own emotional indigestion. Transference is inevitable: a therapist working with women trapped in abusive marriages may unconsciously project her own dependency fears onto her clients. Only by addressing their own unresolved pain can healers model healthy emotional digestion and guide communities toward liberation.

2. Scope and Purpose of the Book

This book integrates psychoanalytic theory, cross-cultural observation, and public health insight to:

- Illuminate the dynamics of emotional indigestion in individuals, families, and communities.
- Show how repression, dependency, and inherited trauma create psychosomatic illness and intergenerational suffering.
- Provide psychoanalytic and practical tools for recognizing, processing, and healing emotional indigestion.
- Highlight the cultural and societal contexts—rural villages, urban centers, traditional healing, and church-based systems—that shape, perpetuate, or alleviate indigestion.

Through case narratives, theory, and reflective exercises, the book is both scholarly and applied. It invites readers to confront what has been swallowed and suppressed, to trace it to its roots, and to transform it into a source of self-awareness, autonomy, and resilience.

Emotional indigestion is a silent epidemic that bridges psychology, sociology, and public health. It is experienced across continents, cultures, and socioeconomic strata. It affects not only those suffering directly but also the communities in which they live, creating a cycle of dependency, repression, and intergenerational trauma.

Drawing on Freud and Jung, informed by field observations and global case studies, this book proposes that liberation is possible—but it requires courage, consciousness, and structured reflection. Healing begins when silence is broken, repression is addressed, and emotional indigestion is fully digested—personally, relationally, and communally.

2. Why this book is relevant for you!

This book is about emotional indigestion—the unprocessed grief, desires, and fears that remain trapped in our bodies, relationships, and communities when we cannot speak or transform them. It takes a psychoanalytic approach, guided by the insights of Sigmund Freud and Carl Jung, while also listening to the rhythms of African traditional healing and the lived experiences of ordinary people across the globe.

Freud showed us that the unconscious is not silent; what we repress always returns, often in disguised forms—through dreams, physical illness, slips of the tongue, or patterns of relationship. His ideas of attachment, repression, transference, and ego dissolution help explain why people repeat the same painful dynamics: why a woman inherits her mother's silence, why a man fears losing his masculinity if he shows weakness, why communities suppress pain through stigma instead of confronting it.

Jung expanded this vision by reminding us that the psyche also carries collective archetypes—shadows that societies project onto others, myths that shape gender roles, and inherited stories that repeat across generations. For Jung, what is not made conscious returns as fate.

Emotional indigestion, in this sense, is not only personal—it is a collective inheritance. Villages, families, and even entire nations carry unresolved psychic wounds.

This book brings Freud and Jung into dialogue with communities in pain—from women in rural African villages to men in European cities, from pastors in Ghana to therapists in New York. It asks:

- How does silence become a symptom?
- How does repressed grief become embodied as illness?

Why do helpers—therapists, pastors, healers—often carry the very indigestion they claim to cure?

How does intergenerational suffering become normalized, until daughters and sons live out the unfinished emotional lives of their parents?

At its core, this book argues that emotional indigestion is both a psychological and a public health problem. Stress and silence contribute to disease burdens in communities, and repression sustains cycles of trauma. Healing requires more than advice or survival—it requires the courage to face unconscious fears, to trace suffering back to its roots, and to create new pathways of freedom.

The book is not only analytical but also practical. It closes each major section with Workbook reflections, offering readers tools to begin digesting their own buried emotions. In this way, it seeks to become more than a text of theory: it aims to be a companion for healing.

Above all, this book is about liberation. It is about reclaiming the right to feel, to speak, to break inherited silences, and to transform what has been repressed into a source of strength. Through Freud's precision, Jung's depth, and the wisdom of communal healing, it invites us to confront our indigestion—and to finally digest what has been buried for too long.

3. Part I: Understanding Emotional Indigestion

Chapter 1: Who Am I Without My Partner?

- We ask ourselves: Who am I in this relationship? Who will I be if I stay? Who will I be if I leave?
- Many attach their self-worth to their partners—depending on them for joy, safety, movement, and even survival.
- Forgetting one's identity leads to dependency syndrome, where happiness is outsourced instead of cultivated from within.

Key Arguments

- Identity often dissolves inside relationships; people define themselves only as "wife," "husband," "partner."
- Dependency syndrome: relying on partners for joy, movement, survival.
- Forgetting selfhood is the root cause of indigestion.

Examples

- A young woman who marries early, forgets her dreams, and later cannot answer the question: "What do you love outside your partner?"
- Villagers saying, "If my husband leaves, I am nothing."

The profound question, "Who am I without my partner?" often emerges as individuals grapple with their identity within and outside of a significant relationship, forcing them to confront "Who am I in this relationship? Who will I be if I stay? Who will I be if I leave?"

For many, self-worth becomes inextricably linked to their significant other, with a deep-seated reliance for elements as fundamental as joy, safety, personal movement, and even a sense of survival. This inadvertent surrender of one's core identity inevitably fosters a dependency syndrome, where the cultivation of personal happiness is tragically outsourced to another, rather than nurtured and sustained from within.

Whose Reflection Is This?

The sun was just beginning to dip behind the horizon, casting a warm amber glow over the quiet village that Sarah had called home for the better part of her life. The familiar hum of cicadas resonated through the air, a lullaby she'd grown up with, yet today it felt distant, almost hollow.

Sarah sat on her porch, clutching a steaming mug, lost in thought. Her eyes flicked to the photograph nestled between her fingers — a picture of her and Marcus, taken just last summer. Their smiles were bright, but beneath that veneer, an unspoken ache lingered. Who am I in this relationship? she wondered silently, her heart heavy with questions.

"It's like I've become a shadow of myself," she whispered aloud, almost surprised at the confession. Marcus approached, leaning against the doorframe, a gentle smile on his face.

"You seem distant tonight," he said softly. "What's on your mind?"

Sarah hesitated, then sighed. "I've been thinking... about us. About who I am when I'm with you. Sometimes I wonder if I've forgotten what I like, what makes me *me."

Marcus looked thoughtful. "I don't want you to forget yourself, Sarah. But I also worry—what happens if you leave? Would you be okay?"

She looked away, a flicker of vulnerability crossing her face. "Who will I be if I stay? And who will I be if I leave?" The words escaped her softly, yet they echoed loudly inside her mind.

Their conversation uncovered a truth neither dared to voice aloud — many attach their self-worth to their partners—depending on them for joy, safety, movement, and even survival. But Sarah knew, deep down, that forgetting one's identity leads to dependency syndrome, a trap where happiness is outsourced instead of cultivated from within.

She took a breath, feeling the weight of her own thoughts. The village was peaceful, but inside her mind, a storm was brewing. She realized that her story was just beginning: a journey to find herself, whether she stayed or left.

As the last rays of sunlight vanished, Sarah looked out into the evening, her heart pounding with newfound clarity. Because the greatest question wasn't about others — it was about discovering the strength to define herself, beyond the reflection of anyone else.

Reflection Questions

1. How would I describe myself if I removed the titles of "wife," "husband," or "partner"?
2. What are my personal dreams or hobbies that I have neglected because of this relationship?

Exercise

- Identity Map: Draw a circle in the middle with your name. Around it, write roles you play (mother, worker, wife, daughter). Then add qualities that are yours regardless of roles (kind, creative, intelligent). Compare which list is longer—roles or qualities?

Reflection Questions

1. When was the last time I felt happy without someone else being the reason?
2. Do I believe I can survive and thrive on my own? Why or why not?

Exercise

- Self-Check: Write down 3 areas of your life where you rely heavily on another person (e.g., happiness, decision-making, finances).
- Then circle one area where you could begin practicing independence.

Reflection Questions

- If I removed my roles (partner, spouse, parent), how would I describe myself?
- What personal dreams or hobbies have I neglected?

Small Step

- Revisit one hobby or passion I left behind, even for 15 minutes this week.

Affirmation

- "I am more than my roles; I am a whole person."

1. Key Lesson I Learned
(Write what emotional indigestion means to you personally.)
2. My Reflection Questions

- Do I see areas in my life where I rely too much on others for happiness?
- Have I forgotten what joy feels like when it comes from me?

3. My Small Step This Week

- Write down 3 moments in the past when I felt happy by

myself.

4. My Affirmation

- "I was whole before; I can be whole again."

5. Notes / Free Writing

(Capture first feelings about emotional indigestion and where you may see it in your life.)

Chronic Disease, Denial, and Environmental Shadows

In many South African communities—whether in the scattered villages of Limpopo, the mining towns of Mpumalanga, or the high-walled suburbs of Gauteng—chronic disease does not arrive as a sudden catastrophe. It creeps in silently, disguised as headaches, sleepless nights, fatigue, or ulcers, until the body cannot contain the weight of repression any longer.

Stroke, hypertension, diabetes, and chronic depression often reveal what has long been denied: that emotional pain, social stress, and toxic environments have fermented inside the psyche and somatized into illness.

Freud's concept of denial (Verleugnung) is not merely a refusal to acknowledge the truth; it is a defense mechanism that allows the ego to survive unbearable realities. People often know—or at least suspect—that the soil of their environment is poisoning them, that the stress of unstable work or fractured family structures is eroding their health, that unspoken grief is eating away at their strength. Yet acknowledging this openly would mean facing overwhelming helplessness. Denial therefore becomes a silent ally, a shield against despair. But the cost is high: emotional indigestion.

Environmental Aspects as Silent Contributors

Consider the woman in rural Mpumalanga who lives near a mine. She coughs persistently, her blood pressure climbs, and she feels constant fatigue. She tells herself, "It is only the dust," while deep down she knows it is also the stress of raising children alone while her husband migrates for work. The mine dust is real, but so is the emotional dust she swallows daily. Her illness is not just environmental, but psychosocial—the product of silence, repression, and fear.

In Limpopo, families who endure drought seasons often speak of hunger with stoic detachment: "It is life." The environment becomes part of the denial. The headaches and ulcers that follow are framed as bad luck, or even witchcraft, rather than as the body's reaction to chronic worry, scarcity, and unexpressed mourning for lost dreams. Here we see

Freud's concept of repression layered onto environmental trauma—the psychic refusal to grieve transforms into bodily symptom.

Among educated professionals in Pretoria, the denial takes another form. They know that long commutes, constant competition, and the pressure of maintaining high social status are fueling hypertension and heart disease. Yet they rationalize: "It is part of success." To admit that the very lifestyle they worked for is damaging their health would collapse the illusion of achievement. Thus, repression converts into silence, and silence into stroke.

Silent Trauma and Emotional Indigestion

The link between environment, denial, and emotional indigestion lies in how communities normalize suffering. When hypertension becomes "just aging," when ulcers are "just stress," when insomnia is laughed off as "thinking too much," society collectively denies the emotional roots of disease. Trauma becomes woven into the environment itself—dust, drought, unemployment, social pressure—and individuals digest it daily, unaware of how it corrodes their bodies.

Freud observed that what the psyche cannot process consciously will return through symptom. In these communities, unprocessed fear of poverty, unspoken grief about failed marriages, and unacknowledged anger toward unjust environments find their voice in chronic disease. Illness becomes the language of repression.

Toward Acknowledgment

Healing requires breaking through denial. This means acknowledging that chronic disease is not only biological, not only environmental, but deeply emotional. It requires courage to say: "This high blood pressure is also my silence. This ulcer is also my grief. This shortness of breath is also my fear." Only then does the possibility of reclaiming selfhood arise—when the hidden connections between environment, psyche, and body are made visible.

In psychoanalytic language, the question "Who am I without my partner?" is not merely a social inquiry; it is a confrontation with the unconscious. Freud teaches us that the human psyche is not transparent to itself. Much of who we are remains buried beneath layers of repression, denial, and unspoken desire. When we enter into relationships—whether arranged, chosen, or imposed—we often place these buried parts of ourselves into the care of the other. The partner becomes not just a companion, but a carrier of identity, desire, and even survival.

Identity Dissolving into Relationship

Freud spoke of the ego as that fragile mediator between inner drives and external reality. Yet in relationships, especially where social or cultural expectations dictate our roles, the ego can collapse into the image of the partner. The young bride in a Limpopo village, married off before she has discovered her own desires, may unconsciously take her husband's dreams as her own. She cooks his favorite meals, tends to his land, raises children under his name—and, slowly, when asked what she loves outside of him, she struggles to answer. Her ego has fused with his.

This is not unique to rural life. In Johannesburg's wealthier suburbs, a woman may enter into a marriage of prestige, where her worth is silently measured by the car she drives, the house she keeps, and the social circles she enters. Outwardly, she appears independent. Yet unconsciously, her sense of "I" remains contingent upon her husband's income, his reputation, and his approval.

Freud might say her ego-ideal—that inner figure of who she wishes to be—has been projected onto her partner. Without him, she fears she will fall into emptiness.

Dependency Syndrome: The Outsourcing of Happiness

Freud's notion of oral fixation—the earliest stage of psychic development—offers a striking metaphor here. At the oral stage, the infant depends entirely on the mother for nourishment. If this dependency is unresolved, the adult may unconsciously repeat it, seeking partners who provide emotional or material sustenance in the same way. We see this vividly in rural communities where women say, "If my husband leaves, I am nothing." The unconscious association is clear: the husband is not only a man, but a substitute for the nurturing breast, a guarantor of survival.

Yet dependency is not limited to poverty. In high-class settings, the dependency may be more subtle but no less powerful. A man who prides himself on being the financial provider may unconsciously believe that without his partner's admiration and reliance, he ceases to exist. His very masculinity becomes dependent on her gaze, much as the infant once depended on the mother's gaze for a sense of being alive.

Forgetting the Self: Emotional Indigestion

Freud often described repression as a pushing down of what is unbearable into the unconscious. In relationships marked by dependency, what is repressed is the self. The young woman with artistic dreams suppresses them, because to pursue them might threaten the marriage arrangement.

The man who wishes to travel, to study further, buries this desire under the weight of his partner's expectations. Over time, these repressed selves do not disappear. They ferment. They gather like undigested food in the psyche, creating what I call emotional indigestion.

The symptoms of this indigestion are familiar: anxiety that seems to appear without cause, irritability toward the partner, a gnawing sense of restlessness. Freud would call these neurotic symptoms—the disguised return of what has been repressed. The truth is that forgetting selfhood is not a neutral act. It is the slow starvation of the inner life, and the body-mind revolts.

Case Illustrations

- Village Example: A widow in Mokopane confesses that she cannot walk to the market alone because for 20 years her husband accompanied her. She has no memory of moving freely by herself, no map of independence. She whispers, "I have forgotten how to be me."
- High-Class Example: A Sandton executive, married into wealth, admits that without her husband's name and networks, she feels invisible in elite spaces. She describes her life as "a borrowed existence."

Examples from Village and City

In a small village in Limpopo, a widow once confessed: "I do not know how to live without him. Even the air feels borrowed." Her words reveal the unconscious fusion of self with other; she cannot breathe as herself because her identity has been consumed by her role as wife. Freud would see in this the collapse of ego boundaries, where the "I" is no longer separate from the "you."

By contrast, in Sandton, a man who divorces after two decades of a prestigious marriage finds himself unable to sit alone in his penthouse. Surrounded by wealth, he feels impoverished, because his sense of self was fed entirely by being the husband of a successful woman. Both the village widow and the city divorcee suffer the same psychic wound: the disappearance of the self beneath the shadow of the partner.

The Path Toward Healing

Healing begins with the analytic act of remembering—bringing to consciousness what has been repressed. Freud believed that the work of analysis is to help the patient put into words what has remained unconscious.

For those suffering from emotional indigestion, the task is to recall forgotten desires, to speak the unspeakable: "I once wanted to study medicine." "I loved singing as a child, but I gave it up." "I stayed silent when I should have spoken."

To rediscover oneself outside the partner is to reclaim the lost fragments of identity. This does not mean rejecting love or companionship, but rather refusing to outsource one's entire being to another. It means cultivating inner joy, inner freedom, and inner safety, rather than making them wholly dependent on someone else's presence.

The unconscious will resist. Fear will whisper: "If I live for myself, I will lose love." But the deeper truth, revealed through analysis, is that only when one reclaims the self can love become authentic—no longer a desperate clinging, but a meeting of two whole beings.

These two women, separated by geography and class, share the same psychic wound: they have substituted their identity with the figure of the partner.

The Shadows of Memory

In the heart of London, amidst the fog and the relentless hum of city life, Dr. Malon sat silently in his cozy yet cluttered office. The walls were lined with shelves bursting with books on psychoanalysis, history, and poetry—reminders of his lifelong pursuit to understand the human psyche. Today, his patient was Jonathan, a man haunted by shadows of his past.

Jonathan's voice trembled as he recounted his latest turmoil. "I just don't understand, Malon. I keep blaming Mooi for everything, but I know deep down—I'm the one who's hurting her. And yet, I can't shake this bitterness." His eyes flickered with frustration and confusion.

Malon nodded gently, encouraging him to continue. "Tell me more about this bitterness. Where do you think it originates from?"

Jonathan took a deep breath. "It's my father. He used to beat my mother, and I saw it all. I promised myself I'd never be like him. But somehow, I've become what I hated. And Mooi... she's just a mirror of my past, isn't she?"

Malon leaned forward, his voice calm but firm. "Remember, Jonathan, *the path toward healing begins with the analytic act of remembering—bringing to consciousness what has been repressed. You've carried this pain for so long, but facing it is the first step."

The session lingered as Jonathan delved into memories long buried. Outside, the London rain tapped gently against the windowpane, a soothing rhythm echoing the slow process of uncovering hidden truths.

Weeks later, Malon found himself reminiscing about his own journey. In a different setting, in his office in Australia, he reflected on a case that had challenged him deeply—the story of Luci, a young woman battling her own internal shadows.

Luci had come from a small town in Mpumalanga, South Africa, where her childhood memories were tinged with silence and unspoken pain. She had moved to London seeking refuge and clarity but found herself tangled in her unresolved trauma.

During their sessions, Luci often spoke of her love for singing as a child—a pure joy she had long suppressed. "I loved singing," she whispered, "but I gave it up because I thought I had to be serious, to be responsible. I thought that's what adults did."

Malon gently prodded. "What happens when you think about that?"

Luci looked away, eyes shimmering with unshed tears. "It's like a door I can't open. I feel like I lost parts of myself, and now I don't even know what I want anymore."

In that moment, Malon realized that reclaiming oneself outside the partner was vital. Reclaiming the lost fragments—those childhood desires, passions, and dreams—was essential for genuine healing.

Meanwhile, in the bustling corridors of the Polokwane Hospital, Maria—a nurse and Malon's former patient—found herself at a crossroads. She had always been a pillar of strength for others but had never confronted her own suppressed memories of her abusive marriage.

Her ex-husband, Jakes, had been a tyrant, his violence leaving scars deeper than the physical. Yet, Maria hid her pain behind a brave facade. When Malon visited her in his capacity as a community therapist, she confided in him.

"I stayed silent when I should have spoken," she admitted softly. "I thought I was protecting my children. But I was just trapping myself in that silence."

Malon nodded, understanding. "Healing begins with the act of remembering. You must speak your truth, Maria. Only then can you begin to reclaim your identity outside the shadow of your past."

In a different realm, in New York, 2025, Jakes—her ex-husband—was grappling with his own demons. His life had spiraled into loneliness and regret. He finally acknowledged that his abusive actions stemmed from his own unresolved trauma, rooted in his childhood in KwaZulu-Natal.

He reached out to Malon, seeking forgiveness—not just from Maria but from himself. Conversations flowed, raw and honest, as Jakes confronted his past. Through these dialogues, he started understanding how his history had shaped his destructive patterns.

Back in London, Malon's office was alive with energy as the city bustled outside. His current patient, Mavis, a teacher struggling with guilt and fractured identity, sat across from him. Mavis shared her story of walking away from her passion for dance after her parents disapproved.

"I once wanted to study medicine," she said, voice thick with emotion. "But I gave it up because I thought I had to be responsible, practical. Now, I feel like I lost myself."

Malon looked at her compassionately. "Sometimes, healing means remembering who we were before the world told us to forget. It's about speaking the unspeakable."

As their sessions continued, Malon saw in Mavis the same journey he had guided many through—a rediscovery of self beyond societal expectations and past wounds.

In the quiet hours of the night, Malon often pondered how different lives intertwined through shared pain and healing. The stories of Jonathan, Luci, Maria, Jakes, and Mavis reflected a universal truth: Healing begins with the analytic act of remembering.

It is a painstaking process of bringing into consciousness what has been repressed—the forgotten desires, the silenced voices, the fragments of identity buried under layers of pain. Only through this act of remembrance can one begin to reclaim themselves outside the partner, outside the trauma.

In the year 2025, as the world faced ongoing upheaval, these stories underscored a timeless truth—that healing is a personal voyage, rooted in memory, courage, and the unyielding hope for renewal.

And in his office, Malon continued to listen, to guide, and to believe—knowing that every story of pain carries within it the seed of healing, waiting to be awakened by the simple yet profound act of remembering.

Workbook Section: Rediscovering Self Beyond the Partner

Reflection Questions

1. What part of myself have I silenced or repressed in my relationship?
2. When I imagine myself alone, who do I become?
3. In what ways has dependency shaped my sense of worth?

Small Step

Write down one activity, dream, or joy that is yours alone—not tied to your partner. Commit to engaging with it this week, even for just 30 minutes.

Affirmation

"I am whole within myself. My worth does not dissolve in the absence of another."

Who Am I Without My Partner?

- Key questions: Who am I in this relationship? Who will I be if I leave?
- How relationships shape personal identity.
- Dependency syndrome: depending on partners for joy, safety, and purpose.
- Forgetting the self: the origin of emotional indigestion.

Fundamentally, the concept of "Emotional Indigestion" encapsulates the profound psychological and emotional distress that emerges when an individual becomes misaligned with their own sense of self, particularly within the context of a meaningful relationship. This persistent discomfort often manifests through the troubling introspective query: "What am I without my partner?"

This is not a passing thought or a casual worry—it is an existential reckoning, a confrontation with the deepest ambiguities of selfhood. At the heart of this struggle lie two piercing questions: "Who am I within this relationship?" and perhaps more daunting, "Who will I be if I leave?" The first compels us to examine the compromises, adaptations, and silences we perform in love—whether our authentic self is being expressed or suppressed. The second forces us to imagine the disorienting emptiness that separation might bring: a life stripped of the familiar rhythm of shared existence, where identity must be rebuilt from fragments.

Relationships, by their very nature, reshape identity. They mold and transform us, often in ways too subtle to notice. We come to define ourselves through our partnerships—through the shared routines, the mutual responsibilities, and the roles we embody. A partner becomes more than a companion; they become a mirror, reflecting back our strengths, insecurities, and blind spots. Over time, the individual "I" dissolves into a collective "we," a fusion that offers belonging but also risks erasing boundaries.

Yet this merging, if left unchecked, can evolve into what might be called dependency syndrome. This is the state in which one unconsciously outsources essential needs—joy, safety, and even purpose—to another person. The partner ceases to be one dimension of life and instead becomes the entire axis of meaning. Self-worth, direction, and emotional stability become tethered not to an inner foundation but to the fragile contingencies of another's presence, attention, or approval.

The hidden danger of such dependency is the gradual forgetting of oneself. Individual passions are neglected, dreams deferred, and inner convictions muted in the attempt to preserve harmony—or simply because the partner's desires eclipse one's own. The "I" shrinks as the "we" expands, until personal identity is hollowed out, its boundaries blurred and its essence diluted.

This self-abandonment—silent, unnoticed, and often justified as "love" or "sacrifice"—is the breeding ground of what we call emotional indigestion. Just as unprocessed food burdens the body, unprocessed feelings and forfeited identities weigh heavily on the psyche. The result is a spiritual discomfort that lingers beneath the surface: a persistent unease, a gnawing sense that something vital has been swallowed but never digested. It is the quiet death of the independent spirit, and the birth of a suffering that speaks not through words but through restlessness, conflict, and even illness.

Chapter 2: The Body Remembers

Emotional Indigestion and Health

Key Arguments

- Emotional pain manifests in the body: stress → illness.
- Hypertension, stroke, ulcers, and depression are often linked to suppressed emotional struggles.
- In rural areas, without access to therapy, people express emotional indigestion through physical sickness.

Examples

- A woman who stayed in an abusive marriage and later suffered recurring strokes.
- A farmer who developed ulcers after years of silently enduring marital conflict.

- Emotional indigestion is not just a metaphor—it manifests in the body.
- Stress, unresolved fear, and emotional dependency contribute to conditions like stroke, high blood pressure, and other chronic illnesses.
- In villages and rural communities, where access to mental health services is limited, these emotional struggles often present as physical disease.

The Body as a Stage for Emotional Indigestion

- Emotional indigestion is far more than a metaphor. It is a lived, embodied reality where the unprocessed contents of the psyche—the fears, shames, and longings that never find words—are swallowed, suppressed, and ultimately lodged within the body. Persistent stress, unresolved fear, and a heavy dependence on others for emotional security become too large to contain in the unconscious alone. They spill over into the body, where they script their suffering in strokes, hypertension, diabetes, ulcers, and a range of chronic conditions. What Freud described as the return of the repressed is vividly alive here: what cannot be spoken, mourned, or acknowledged consciously returns in another form—symptom.

- In rural Limpopo or Mpumalanga, the somatic expression of emotional pain is even more pronounced. Without accessible therapists, psychoanalysts, or even consistent primary health care, villagers must hold their grief and anxiety privately. A woman abandoned by her husband after decades of marriage cannot speak freely of her despair because cultural narratives shame her into silence: "Endure for the children," "A wife must remain strong," or "Prayer will heal the wound." She represses her rage and swallows her loneliness, but the body refuses silence. Soon, she suffers her first stroke—explained away by the community as "God's will," yet in truth a testimony of decades of indigested pain.
- Similarly, a farmer enduring years of marital conflict without ever naming his hurt develops chronic ulcers. To his neighbors, the ulcers are simply "a sickness of the stomach." To psychoanalytic eyes, however, they are a stomach burning with words that could never be spoken—resentments, humiliations, and fears of inadequacy that the unconscious redirects into the body.

The Mechanism of Emotional Indigestion

- Freud taught us that repression shields the ego from unbearable truths, but it does not eliminate them. Instead, the repressed content finds another outlet. In contexts of poverty and silence, the outlet is the body itself. Persistent stress activates the nervous system, keeping the body in a state of vigilance. The heart beats faster, blood pressure rises, digestion falters. Fear of abandonment, though never spoken aloud, signals the body to tense against anticipated loss. Dependency on a partner, though denied in words, becomes visible in headaches, fatigue, and shortness of breath whenever that partner withdraws affection.
- Emotional indigestion is thus a cycle: unspoken pain → repression → chronic tension → physical disease. What begins as a psychological defense becomes a medical condition.

Starkness in Rural Communities

- The scarcity of mental health resources in rural communities sharpens this phenomenon. In Pretoria, an educated professional might at least name her panic attacks, or seek temporary relief from a psychologist. In Ga-Mphahlele or Bushbuckridge, a woman waking at night with pounding heartbeats has no such vocabulary. Instead, she interprets her panic as "a bad spirit" or as simply fatigue from hard work. This mislabeling, itself a form of denial, deepens the repression. The body becomes the only diary in which her trauma is written.

- The silence is communal, not only individual. Villages teach people to keep their hurts private, lest they bring shame to the family. Men in North West who feel emasculated by unemployment cannot speak of their despair, for masculinity is culturally tied to providing. Their silence breeds ulcers, strokes, and chronic headaches. Women enduring arranged marriages cannot confess their longing for freedom without risking expulsion from family networks. Their grief turns inward, tightening blood vessels, raising blood pressure, and marking their bodies with disease.

Emotional Indigestion Across Class Lines

- One might assume that wealth buffers against such somatic suffering, yet emotional indigestion crosses all class lines. A politician's wife in Sandton remains in an abusive marriage not out of love, but out of fear of public humiliation and loss of social standing. She represses her terror, smiling at galas, only to collapse later with hypertension. A businessman clings to his wife not because of affection, but because she represents prestige. His identity is fused with her presence, and the unconscious fear of losing status manifests as chest pain and insomnia.
- Both the poor villager and the wealthy socialite embody the same truth: emotional indigestion unravels the body when the psyche is forbidden to speak.

The Irony of Silence

- What is most tragic is the irony: repression is meant to protect the self from unbearable awareness, but it becomes the very mechanism of destruction. Silence feels like strength, but it eats away from within. The mind says, "I cannot afford to feel this," and so the body feels it instead. The woman who cannot speak her rage bleeds it into her arteries. The man who cannot voice his shame burns it into his stomach lining. Emotional indigestion is therefore not a metaphorical concept but the most faithful diary of repressed life—the body itself becoming the page where trauma is recorded.

Emotional Digestion - Case

The city hummed with relentless energy, neon lights flickering against the midnight sky as Kira navigated her crowded subway train. Her mind, however, was miles away—caught in a swirl of worries she couldn't quite name. She rubbed her temple absentmindedly, feeling the faint throb behind her eyes, a familiar pain that had become her constant companion over the past few months.

In her urban world, stress was an invisible weight, pressing down relentlessly, yet rarely acknowledged. She often thought, I should relax more, but the city's demands seemed insatiable. Her phone buzzed—a message from her mother back in the village. Kira hesitated, then read it aloud: "Are you eating well? Remember, emotional peace is just as important."

A faint smile flickered on her lips. Somehow, her mother's words felt both comforting and distant. But beneath her calm exterior, a storm raged. She had been feeling increasingly anxious, her chest tight at times, her thoughts racing. Her body was a battlefield, her stress manifesting in headaches and exhaustion.

Later that evening, in her tiny apartment, Kira sat on her balcony gazing at the sprawling city lights. Her phone buzzed again, this time a call from her grandmother.

"Kira, my child," came the warm voice, "You carry so much within you. Sometimes, the worries and fears we hide become heavy, like a stone in the stomach."

Kira chuckled softly. "I guess I never thought of it that way, grandma."

"Emotional indigestion," her grandmother said gently. "It's not just a metaphor. When our hearts are troubled, it shows up in our bodies. Stress, unresolved fears, dependencies—these all can lead to illness, even strokes or high blood pressure, especially when we ignore what our spirits need to heal."

Kira paused, absorbing her words. She looked out over the city's maze of lights, feeling a strange kinship with the distant villages she often visited as a child. In those quiet, rural communities, mental health wasn't talked about openly, but the effects were palpable. People carried their burdens deep inside, and sometimes, these burdens turned into physical pain or disease.

Suddenly, she remembered her cousin's story—how her uncle had suffered a stroke, not just from physical causes but from decades of unspoken fears and emotional suppression.

"So, you're saying," Kira whispered into the night, "that what we keep inside can make us sick?"

"Exactly," her grandmother replied softly. "Healing begins when we acknowledge what we feel, not just what we see on the surface. Emotional digestion is vital—lest our bodies become the silent victims of what we refuse to face."

As the city's hum persisted, Kira felt a flicker of understanding. The bustling urban life had pushed her away from her own emotional needs, but perhaps, now, she would start to listen—both to herself and to the quiet voices from her roots. The journey toward healing, she realized, might begin with simply acknowledging the emotional indigestion she'd long ignored.

Reflection Questions

1. How would I describe myself if I removed the titles of "wife," "husband," or "partner"?
2. What are my personal dreams or hobbies that I have neglected because of this relationship?

Exercise

- Identity Map: Draw a circle in the middle with your name. Around it, write roles you play (mother, worker, wife, daughter). Then add qualities that are yours regardless of roles (kind, creative, intelligent). Compare which list is longer—roles or qualities?

The Body Remembers

Reflection Questions

1. How does my body react when I am stressed in my relationship? (Headaches, stomach pain, fatigue?)
2. Do I believe my physical health is connected to my emotions?

Exercise

- Body Scan Journal: For one week, track moments of stress or conflict and note the body's reaction. At the end, review patterns.

Reflection Questions

- How does my body react to stress in my relationship?
- Do I see a link between my emotions and my physical health?

Small Step

- Keep a daily log of body signals when I feel stressed.

Affirmation

- "My body speaks the truth, and I will listen."

The Body as a Stage for Repression

Freud often reminded us that when the psyche cannot speak, the body will. He referred to this as conversion—psychic energy that has been repressed finds a pathway into bodily symptoms. What is silenced in words returns in headaches, ulcers, or trembling hands. This process is not metaphorical—it is psycho-somatic reality.

In many South African contexts, particularly rural villages, the body becomes the first language of pain because access to therapy, psychoanalysis, or even a space to talk is absent. A Limpopo mother who cannot tell anyone of her loneliness after her children migrate to Johannesburg begins to complain of constant chest pain. The clinic finds no clear cardiac pathology, yet her symptoms persist. Freud would remind us: what has been repressed returns disguised. Her heartache is literalized.

In both poverty and privilege, the same law of the unconscious applies: emotional indigestion will not remain hidden. When the psyche cannot digest what has been swallowed—trauma, silence, dependency—it ferments in the body until illness manifests.

Emotional Pain and Physical Illness

The link between unresolved emotional pain and chronic illness is not speculative. In Freud's early case studies—such as Anna O.—the hysterical symptoms of paralysis and cough were traced back to unprocessed trauma. Modern medicine now names these "psychosomatic" conditions. Hypertension, stroke, ulcers, and depression often emerge where long-term emotional conflict has been repressed.

- Stress → Hypertension: Constant anxiety about survival, children, or marital conflict keeps the nervous system aroused, constricting vessels, raising blood pressure.
- Suppressed Rage → Stroke: Repressed anger, particularly in relationships where cultural norms silence women, can culminate in strokes. The blocked words and emotions erupt in the body's circulation.
- Chronic Worry → Ulcers: When fear and shame are chewed over but never spoken, the stomach burns. Freud's term "conversion" is lived out in the gut.
- Isolation → Depression: In both rural villages and wealthy suburbs, when longing, grief, or desire is buried, the ego turns that pain inward, resulting in withdrawal, hopelessness, and despair.

Village Realities: Limpopo and Mpumalanga

In Limpopo's villages, a woman stays in an abusive marriage because divorce is condemned by tradition and the church. She silences her humiliation for decades. Later, she suffers recurring strokes. The medical team treats the brain, but the underlying repression—the years of swallowed shame—remains unspoken. Her body was the only vessel through which her truth could emerge.

In Mpumalanga, a farmer suppresses his rage at being financially controlled by his wife's family. For years he works in silence, drinking heavily but never speaking his resentment. At 52, he develops severe ulcers, his stomach lining eaten away by the acids of unspoken rage. His illness is not only biological; it is psychoanalytic—it is the unconscious seeking expression.

These stories are not isolated. In the North West, young men who feel emasculated by poverty, unable to provide for their families, often present with chest pain or fainting spells. Lacking the language to articulate psychic suffering, they turn instead to alcohol, violence, or withdrawal. The repression of inadequacy becomes symptom.

High-Class Society: Silence Behind Glass Walls

In Johannesburg's wealthy suburbs, emotional indigestion takes a different form. A Sandton executive in her 40s endures a loveless marriage because divorce would damage her social image. She tells no one of the emptiness she feels, yet she visits her doctor monthly with headaches and rising blood pressure. Her body becomes her diary.

Similarly, a lawyer in Pretoria, educated and financially secure, develops chronic migraines after years of pretending to be the "perfect husband." His repression is not born of poverty but of performance—the superego demands a mask of success and stability. Freud would call this the tyranny of the superego, punishing the ego with symptoms when forbidden feelings—anger, despair, desire—cannot be spoken.

The same unconscious dynamics that shape rural women's strokes shape high-class migraines. What differs is the external context—culture, money, education—but not the psychic law.

Emotional Indigestion Is Not Just a Metaphor

Freud argued that the repressed is indestructible—it will find a return. When villagers describe being "sick from stress," they are not speaking loosely. They are testifying to the conversion of emotional indigestion into somatic illness.

The body becomes both the battlefield and the messenger. A tightened jaw holds unspoken rage. A stiff back carries the weight of suppressed grief. High blood pressure measures the pulse of unvoiced fears. The stomach ulcer is the burning hunger of unmet needs.

Whether in the clay huts of Limpopo, the farms of Mpumalanga, the mining towns of North West, or the gated communities of Sandton—the law of repression and return applies universally.

Toward Healing: Making the Unconscious Speak

Freud believed that healing begins with making the unconscious conscious. What is repressed must be given words. In practice, this means creating spaces where silence can be broken—whether through therapy, community dialogue, or even personal journaling.

For the woman in Limpopo, speaking the shame of her abusive marriage could be as healing as any medicine. For the Sandton executive, admitting her emptiness could lower her blood pressure more than pills alone. For the Mpumalanga farmer, naming his resentment could soothe his ulcers.

The act of giving voice transforms repression into integration. Instead of the body carrying the burden, the psyche begins to metabolize what was swallowed. This is the true digestion of emotions—the transformation of pain into speech, insight, and ultimately freedom.

Workbook Section: Digesting Pain Before It Becomes Illness

Reflection Questions

1. Where in my body do I feel stress or tension most strongly? What might that part of my body be trying to say?
2. What emotions have I swallowed in silence because I feared judgment, shame, or rejection?
3. If my illness could speak, what words would it say to me today?

Small Step

Write down one unspoken feeling you have carried silently—anger, grief, or fear. Share it in a safe space: with a trusted friend, a journal, or in prayer. Notice how your body feels after expressing it.

Affirmation

"My body is not my enemy. It carries my truth until I am ready to speak it. Today, I choose to listen."

The Body Remembers

- Emotional indigestion as a root cause of chronic illness.
- Stress, anxiety, and unresolved dependency linked to conditions like stroke, hypertension, ulcers.
- Case reflections: how emotions translate into "hidden diseases."
- Why rural communities report illnesses rooted in emotional struggles.

The well-known saying "The Body Remembers" captures a truth that medicine and psychology continue to rediscover: our bodies and minds cannot be separated. What we suppress emotionally often finds expression physiologically. Unresolved traumas, silenced grief, or chronic fear do not simply disappear with time. Instead, they lodge themselves in the body's systems, quietly influencing health in ways that can remain invisible until they erupt as illness.

At the center of this lies the idea of emotional indigestion—a state in which powerful feelings are swallowed but never digested. Emotions such as anger, grief, fear, and dependency, when unacknowledged or unexpressed, remain trapped within the psyche, forcing the body to carry their weight. Over time, this emotional backlog keeps the nervous system locked in a cycle of alarm, flooding the body with stress hormones such as cortisol and adrenaline. This chronic activation of the "fight, flight, or freeze" response disrupts equilibrium, leading to inflammation, nervous system dysregulation, hormonal imbalance, and a weakened immune defense. In this sense, emotional indigestion is not merely a metaphor but a biological reality—a root cause that undermines the body's natural healing ability and lays the groundwork for chronic disease.

The links are striking. Prolonged stress and anxiety place a relentless burden on the cardiovascular system, keeping blood vessels constricted and the heart in overdrive. The result is hypertension, arterial damage, and, eventually, increased risk of stroke.

Anxiety and fear, when lived as a daily condition, disrupt digestive processes, increasing gastric acid production and contributing to painful ulcers. Even dependency—the deep emotional reliance on another for validation or security—creates an internal pressure cooker. Living with the constant fear of abandonment or disapproval traps the individual in a state of hyper-vigilance, straining the heart, tightening the gut, and exhausting the nervous system. What looks like stroke, ulcers, or unexplained chest pain may often be the physical echo of long-silenced emotions.

Therapists and healthcare workers frequently encounter these "hidden diseases." Fibromyalgia, chronic fatigue, irritable bowel syndrome, recurring migraines, and even certain skin conditions often resist conventional treatments. Their persistence baffles medical professionals, until a deeper exploration of the patient's story reveals buried grief, childhood trauma, or ongoing relational strain. The body, unable to find words, becomes the storyteller. Pain, fatigue, or inflammation become its language—a somatic script through which unresolved emotions demand recognition.

In rural communities, this dynamic takes on an even sharper edge. Illnesses linked to emotional distress are particularly visible where cultural, social, and systemic barriers prevent emotional expression. Stoicism is often the cultural norm—people are taught to endure silently, to present strength even when crumbling inside. Admitting to depression, grief, or anxiety can be stigmatized as weakness, and so people translate their anguish into something more socially acceptable: back pain, headaches, stomach trouble, or high blood pressure. Physical ailments carry less shame than confessing to emotional vulnerability.

But this silence comes at a high cost. In villages and rural areas, access to professional mental health care is rare, leaving individuals with almost no outlets for emotional processing. Economic hardship, unemployment, social isolation, and the pressure of judgment from tightly bound communities further compound stress. What might begin as unprocessed grief or fear eventually embeds itself as chronic illness.

A farmer with persistent fatigue, a grandmother with hypertension, or a teenager with chronic stomach problems may, in fact, be carrying the unspoken weight of loss, poverty, or relational conflict.

In these ways, the body becomes both messenger and battleground. When emotions are denied language, they surface as disease. Emotional indigestion, left untreated, corrodes not only psychological balance but also physical resilience, forcing us to confront a sobering truth: healing cannot be achieved by medicine alone. To restore health, we must also tend to the emotions that live, often painfully, inside the body.

Part II: Relationships and Dependency

Chapter 3: Women Trapped in Dependency

Key Arguments

- Arranged marriages remove choice → emotional indigestion grows.
- Financial dependency locks women in unhappy marriages.
- Returning to their family homes is often impossible due to poverty, overcrowding, or lack of parental support.

Examples

- A woman married at 18 for "security" but now trapped with an abusive husband because she is unemployed.
- A girl married off for bride-price, now suffering illness but unable to leave.

Women, Marriage, and Dependency

•Many women are trapped in marriages they did not choose—arranged unions, marriages for financial survival, or marriages sustained by cultural expectation.

•Without education, employment, or social support, leaving becomes impossible. The fear of poverty outweighs the pain of staying.

•Returning "home" is often not an option—there may be no home to return to, or poverty and overcrowding make it unsustainable.

The nexus of women, marriage, and profound dependency presents an extraordinarily complex and often intractable challenge for therapeutic assistance, frequently manifesting as deep-seated emotional 'indigestion' – a chronic, systemic blockage of the spirit that is exceedingly difficult to diagnose, address, and ultimately resolve.

Many women find themselves profoundly immobilised within marital bonds they had little to no genuine agency in choosing. These are not merely unions of convenience, but often arrangements dictated by a myriad of external pressures:

> ◈ Arranged Unions: These may be pre-destined by family tradition, deeply ingrained cultural practices, or a perceived duty to honor familial obligations, often decided without the woman's meaningful consent or even awareness from a young age. Her individual desires, aspirations, and emotional well-being are frequently superseded by collective and patriarchal expectations.

> ◈ Marriages for Financial Survival: For countless women, marriage is not a choice of companionship or love, but the

sole available pathway to economic security, particularly in societies where independent female employment is scarce, stigmatized, or pays poverty wages. It becomes a desperate necessity to escape destitution, secure basic needs, or provide for existing children, effectively trading personal autonomy for material subsistence.

◈ Marriages Sustained by Cultural Expectation: Beyond formal arrangement, societal norms and the unyielding grip of cultural expectations can bind women to undesirable unions. The pervasive fear of social ostracization, the indelible stigma of divorce or single motherhood, and the pressure to uphold family 'honor' can coerce women into enduring unhappy or abusive marriages, making departure a social, familial, and personal impossibility in terms of perceived reputation and acceptance.

Crucially, without fundamental access to education, viable employment opportunities, or robust social support networks, the prospect of leaving such marriages becomes virtually impossible. The systemic barriers are formidable:

◈ Lack of Education: Many women are denied educational opportunities, or their education is curtailed, leaving them without the foundational skills necessary for gainful employment in a competitive market.

◈ Lack of Employment: Even with education, women often face discriminatory hiring practices, limited job availability, or industries that pay wages insufficient to support themselves or dependants, thus perpetuating their economic vulnerability.

◈ Lack of Social Support: The absence of a safety net – be it accessible shelters, financially stable friends, or family willing to offer unconditional support without judgment – isolates them further. They are left without the practical, emotional, or financial infrastructure needed to rebuild a life post-separation.

In this precarious balance, the stark, rational fear of destitution, homelessness, or even the loss of their children, consistently and overwhelmingly outweighs the palpable pain of remaining in an untenable situation. The known torment of their present reality, however agonizing, is often perceived as less terrifying than the unknown, terrifying abyss of total poverty and social abandonment.

Furthermore, the option of returning "home" is frequently non-existent or deeply problematic. For many, there is simply no physical or emotional safe haven to return to; the family home may literally no longer exist, or it may itself be steeped in poverty, overcrowding, or even be a source of further abuse or judgment.

Laying additional burden on already strained households, particularly in collectivist cultures where resources are minimal, can be seen as an unbearable imposition. This lack of a viable 'exit strategy' outside the marriage profoundly cements their reliance, turning any potential path to emotional healing into an excruciatingly slow, arduous, and deeply nuanced process that extends far beyond individual psychological distress, touching upon systemic inequalities and profound societal limitations.

Case study

The city hummed awake, glass towers reflecting the first golden rays of dawn as Maya sat by her small window, her eyes tracing the skyline that seemed both vibrant and distant. The streets below bustled with life—vendors shouting, cars honking, and the rhythmic pulse of an urban heart she was supposed to be part of but often felt alien to.

Today, like every other day, she clothed herself in a quiet silence, masking the ache of a life she didn't choose. Her marriage had been arranged when she was barely eighteen—an unspoken bargain between families she hardly knew. Marriage, they said, would bring security, respect. It would give her a home. But her home now was a cramped apartment in the suburbs, filled with the scent of stale air and unspoken fears.

Maya's husband, Arjun, was already up, shuffling around in the tiny kitchen. The smell of burnt toast wafted in as he called out, "Breakfast's ready." She responded softly, not wanting to disturb the fragile quiet they maintained.

She hesitated before stepping into the kitchen. Her voice was barely above a whisper. "Arjun, do you think... when will things get better?"

He looked at her, momentarily caught off guard. "Better? You mean, for us? I don't know, Maya. We do what we have to." His tone was tired but resigned, a reflection of years spent navigating the weight of unspoken obligations.

Maya's eyes drifted to her reflection in the small mirror on the wall. She saw a young woman—eyes full of dreams, yet now clouded by resignation. Many women are trapped in marriages they did not choose— arranged unions, marriages for financial survival, or marriages sustained by cultural expectation. The chains of dependency tighten quietly, unbreakable by the faintest hope for escape.

Her mind drifted to her childhood village, where dreams of a different life had once danced vividly. But leaving was impossible—no education, no job, no social support to lean on. The fear of poverty and shame was heavier than the pain of staying.

She remembered her mother's words, spoken in hushed tones. "In our world, a woman's place is with her husband. To leave is to bring shame." And so, Maya had stayed, silent and resigned, her aspirations buried beneath layers of obligation.

Later that evening, sitting alone on the balcony, she gazed at the city lights flickering like distant stars. Her phone buzzed—a message from her childhood friend, Leela.

"Are you okay?" it read.

Maya's fingers hovered over her screen, a surge of longing and despair flooding her. What could she say? That she felt trapped within these walls, her own life a shadow of what it could have been?

A tear escaped and traced its silent journey down her cheek. She whispered softly into the night, "Is this all there is?"

In this sprawling city, amidst the glitz and grind, Maya's story was just one of many—women caught in the silent, suffocating grip of dependency, yearning for freedom they dare not speak aloud.

And somewhere deep inside, a flicker of hope began to stir, fragile yet persistent. The question lingered—how long before she found the courage to break free?

Reflection Questions

1. What fears keep me in this relationship? (Money, family expectations, shelter?)
2. If I had all the resources I needed, would I stay?

Exercise

- Safety Net List: Write down people, organizations, or skills you could lean on if you ever needed to leave. Even if the list is short, it's a starting point for building alternatives.

Women Trapped in Dependency

- Arranged marriages and lack of choice.
- Financial dependency as a barrier to freedom.
- The "no return" dilemma: why many women cannot go home.
- Poverty, overcrowded homes, and absence of alternatives.

Many women live confined within a complex web of dependency that touches every aspect of their existence, beginning with a lack of autonomy over their own choices. At the heart of this confinement lies the practice of arranged marriages, where young women are often given little—if any—voice in deciding who they will spend their lives with.

Cultural traditions, familial expectations, and social obligations frequently outweigh their personal dreams, leaving their futures predetermined and binding them to the structures of their marital households. In such settings, individuality is often eclipsed by the broader priorities of family honour, stability, or alliances, forcing women into relationships not necessarily aligned with their emotional or personal needs.

This absence of choice is deepened by financial dependency, one of the most powerful reinforcers of inequality. Many women are systematically excluded from equal access to education, vocational skills, or independent sources of income. Even when opportunities to work exist, restrictive cultural norms, spousal control, or household responsibilities often prevent them from participating fully in the workforce or managing their own finances. As a result, they remain economically tethered to their husbands or in-laws. Without financial independence, the very thought of leaving an unhappy or abusive marriage becomes nearly impossible. The cost of escape is not just emotional—it is existential.

The dilemma becomes even more acute with the looming reality of the "no return" barrier. For many women, leaving a marital home carries profound consequences, both personal and social. Divorce or separation is not merely a private decision—it is a public scandal, often interpreted as failure or shame. Families of origin may reject a daughter who seeks to return, fearing that her decision tarnishes their reputation and standing in the community. The fear of ostracism, judgment, and rejection from one's own family becomes a heavy psychological chain, keeping women in place even when circumstances are intolerable.

Even if a woman finds the courage to resist social stigma, harsh practical realities often block her path. Returning to her natal home may mean facing deep poverty, overcrowding, and households already strained by survival struggles. With little space, few resources, and no infrastructure for reintegration, she risks becoming an additional burden on an already struggling family. In many contexts, the absence of robust safety nets—such as women's shelters, government support, or reliable community programs—further eliminates pathways to safety and autonomy.

Caught in this cycle, women are left with few genuine choices. Dependency is not just emotional—it is structural, cultural, and systemic. Each layer, whether it is financial, social, or familial, reinforces the others, creating an almost inescapable reality. What emerges is not simply individual suffering, but an intergenerational cycle of entrapment, where the lack of alternatives keeps women tied to marriages that diminish their autonomy, silence their voices, and undermine their well-being. Breaking free from this web, in the absence of radical social and structural change, remains a daunting task—one that requires far more than individual resilience, but the transformation of the very systems that sustain dependency.

Chapter 4: Emotional Indigestion Beyond Poverty

Key Arguments

- Wealth does not protect against indigestion—it reshapes it.
- Wealthier women remain trapped by fear of losing lifestyle, respect, or social standing.
- Men and women both struggle with the shame of "falling back" to a lower status.

Examples

- A politician's wife who cannot leave despite abuse because she fears public humiliation.
- A businessman who clings to his wife not out of love, but because she symbolizes prestige.

Emotional Indigestion Across Classes

- Poor women remain in unhealthy marriages because they cannot afford to leave.
- Wealthier women remain because they fear losing status, lifestyle, or social standing.
- In both cases, people stay—not out of love, but out of fear of going back to "less."
- Men, too, experience emotional indigestion, associating their partners with class, respect, or identity, and refusing to let go.

The concept of "Emotional Indigestion Across Classes" aptly describes the pervasive, yet often unacknowledged, discomfort that arises when individuals remain in relationships that no longer serve their emotional well-being, primarily due to factors external to love or genuine connection. This phenomenon transcends socioeconomic barriers, manifesting in distinct yet equally binding ways:

For poor women, the decision to endure unhealthy marriages is often a stark calculation of survival. They remain trapped not out of affection, but because the economic alternative—leaving—presents an unbearable precipice of precarity. The fear is not of "lesser" luxury, but of absolute destitution: the inability to secure independent housing, provide basic necessities like food and clothing for themselves and their children, or access essential services like childcare and healthcare without their partner's support. They may lack the education, job skills, or a robust social safety net to imagine a viable independent future.

The "unhealthy marriage" might encompass emotional neglect, verbal abuse, or even physical violence, but the perceived safety of a roof over their head, however precarious, often outweighs the profound emotional and physical toll of staying. Their indigestible truth is that freedom comes at an unaffordable price.

Conversely, wealthier women navigating equally anemic or toxic partnerships face a different, albeit similarly powerful, set of deterrents. Their chains are often gilded. The resistance to leaving stems from a deep-seated fear of losing the tangible markers of their elevated status: the sprawling home, luxury travel, designer wardrobe, elite social circles, private school for children, and the perceived ease of a life underpinned by significant financial resources. Beyond the material, the fear of a decline in social standing and the associated loss of identity are profound. Being "Mrs. [Prominent Name]" often confers a specific social value and purpose, and divorce threatens to strip away this carefully constructed public persona, potentially inviting judgment, pity, or social ostracization within their insular communities. For them, emotional indigestion is the constant gnawing realization that they are living a beautifully packaged lie, sacrificing authenticity for a comfortable, yet emotionally barren, existence.

In both these scenarios, the underlying commonality is a chilling departure from love as the primary motivator for remaining in a relationship. Instead, individuals stay because of an overwhelming fear of regression—of going back to "less." For the poor, "less" means a descent into abject poverty and insecurity.

For the wealthy, "less" implies a significant drop in privilege, comfort, and social capital. It's a calculated decision where the known, albeit painful, present is deemed preferable to an unknown future perceived as diminished. This internal calculus creates a chronic state of emotional indigestion, a gnawing dissatisfaction that is never fully processed because the perceived external costs of addressing it are too high.

This complex web of fear and perceived loss is not exclusive to women. Men, too, experience their own brand of emotional indigestion within unsatisfactory partnerships. For many men, their partner is inextricably linked to their own sense of identity, class perception, and public respectability. A wife might be seen as a crucial component of their successful image—whether as a "trophy wife" elevating their social standing, a domestic anchor providing stability, or simply as a necessary component of a "complete" family unit in the eyes of society.

The thought of divorce can trigger fears of losing access to social circles, public respect, or even an internal sense of purpose and structure. The partner becomes an integral part of their personal brand, a symbol of achievement or conformity. Consequently, despite a lack of emotional connection or genuine happiness, these men may refuse to let go, unwilling to dismantle the public identity they've meticulously built or face the perceived societal "demotion" that often accompanies separation. Their emotional discomfort is swallowed whole, a bitter pill ensuring the continuation of a relationship that serves their external validation more than their internal peace

Case study

The city never slept, but sometimes it felt like it was holding its breath—waiting, watching. In the shadowed corners of urban life, beneath the glow of neon signs and the hum of traffic, stories of quiet desperation unfolded daily.

Marina sat on her tiny balcony overlooking a bustling boulevard, her fingers trembling as she clutched a faded photograph. The edges had worn soft from years of handling, much like her own resolve. Her marriage was like a slow poison—unhealthy, suffocating—and yet she stayed. The weight of her poverty pressed down on her shoulders, making escape feel like an impossible dream. "I can't afford to leave," she murmured to herself, voice barely audible over the city's din.

Inside the cramped apartment, her husband, Raj, was sprawled on the battered sofa, eyes fixed on the flickering television. He looked up, sensing her agitation. "Are you crying again?" he asked, his tone edged with frustration and something darker—perhaps guilt or indifference.

“No, just tired,” Marina whispered, forcing a smile. “It's nothing.”

Across town, in a sleek high-rise apartment that glittered with chandeliers and designer furniture, Eliza adjusted her pearls in the mirror, her life a stark contrast to Marina's—but the ache was familiar. For her, leaving wasn't an option either. The fear of losing her social standing clung to her like a second skin. She glanced at her reflection, then at her phone, where her best friend texted about their upcoming brunch.

"I can't imagine losing this," she whispered aloud, her voice trembling slightly. "All of this. The status, the respect, the life I've built."

Her husband, Richard, entered the room, offering a glass of wine. "You look beautiful," he said softly, but there was a coldness behind his words.

"Thank you," Eliza replied, forcing politeness. "I just don't want to disappoint anyone."

Both women, despite their differences in circumstance, were bound by a common thread: people stay—not out of love, but out of fear of going back to "less."

Meanwhile, in a dimly lit corner of a downtown bar, Marcus, a middle-aged man with lines etched deep into his face, nursed his drink. His relationship with his wife, Clara, was marked by unspoken resentments. "I can't let her go," he muttered under his breath. "She's the only thing keeping me anchored to my identity."

Clara sat alone across from him, her eyes distant. "You're not the man I married," she said softly.

"Neither am I," Marcus admitted. "But I can't admit that—not to her, not to myself. It's easier to pretend we're still whole than face the emptiness that's crept in."

In this city, under the glow of skyscrapers and the shadows of alleyways, men, women, and even the silent ghosts of their fears, all grapple with their own versions of emotional indigestion. They cling to what they think defines them—status, respect, identity—fearing that losing it would mean losing themselves entirely.

And so, they stay—because sometimes, the hardest part of love isn't letting go, but swallowing the bitter taste of what's comfortable and familiar, even when it chokes the soul.

Reflection Questions

1. Have I ever stayed in a relationship for lifestyle or status, not love?

2. What do I fear losing more: the relationship or the lifestyle it provides?

Exercise

- Lifestyle Audit: Write down your current "comforts" (e.g., house, car, travel). Then list the simple joys you had before (e.g., laughter with friends, walking, gardening). Reflect: which set brings real joy?

Emotional Indigestion Beyond Poverty

Psychoanalytic Expansion

Freud's lens teaches us that wealth does not shield the psyche from conflict—it only disguises it in new forms. Emotional indigestion, that state in which repressed fears and longings ferment within the unconscious, transcends class. A woman in a Limpopo village who remains in an arranged marriage out of financial dependence and a politician's wife in Pretoria who fears the public shame of leaving both drink from the same poisoned well: repression of the self for the preservation of safety.

In Freud's theory, attachment operates not only in infancy but in adult life, where the ego fuses with the partner, the family, or even the idea of social respectability. The unconscious drives the individual to cling, even when the relationship is destructive, because the dissolution of that bond feels like the dissolution of the self.

Attachment and Ego Dissolution

In rural Limpopo, young women often enter marriages arranged by family elders. The girl who once imagined herself as a nurse or teacher discovers years later that she cannot answer the question, "What do you love outside your partner?" Here, attachment collapses into dependency: her ego dissolves into the role of "wife," and her individual identity becomes unrecognizable, even to herself.

In the high-class suburbs of Pretoria, the form is different but the essence is the same. A professional woman, admired for her education, remains in an abusive marriage not because she lacks money to leave but because her identity is bound to the status of "Mrs. X," the politician's wife. Here ego dissolution is not into the family role alone, but into the symbolic prestige of a marriage that upholds her public image.

Freud would call this repression of the id's yearning for freedom. The unconscious knows the truth—"I want to leave, I want to breathe"—but the ego silences it, fearing the collapse of the social mask.

Repression and the Body

Across Mpumalanga's semi-rural towns, women carry repression in their bodies. A farmer's wife, who has endured decades of infidelity in silence, begins to suffer migraines and ulcers. She interprets them as "the price of marriage," not realizing they are the somatic voice of unspoken grief. Freud described repression as psychic energy forced inward; when there is no safe outlet for speech, the body itself becomes the site of confession.

In North West, men too embody repression in their struggle with masculinity. A man who measures his worth only through cattle, land, or political connections finds himself unable to face the loss of a wife who has emotionally withdrawn. She represents not only a partner but his masculine authority. To lose her would be to lose the external symbol of his power. Instead of mourning, he represses, becoming restless, aggressive, or physically ill.

Transference and Class

Transference, in Freud's sense, is when unconscious feelings are displaced onto another figure. In these contexts, relationships become less about love and more about projection.

- The wealthy businessman clings to his wife not out of affection but because she has become the projection of his success. Her presence transfers his unconscious need for prestige onto a human being. To lose her would feel like the collapse of his empire.
- The poor woman in Mpumalanga transfers her longing for parental protection onto her husband. Even when he becomes abusive, she continues to treat him as the father who ensures her survival. Leaving him would mean reawakening the terror of childhood abandonment.

Transference explains why so many remain in relationships that erode them. It is not the partner they cannot leave—it is the unconscious figure their partner represents.

Emotional Indigestion Across Classes

Whether in villages or gated estates, people stay in unhealthy unions not out of love but out of fear. For the poor, fear of hunger. For the wealthy, fear of humiliation. For men across classes, fear of emasculation.

The unconscious, however, does not respect these rationalizations. It pushes its truth forward through dreams, through anxiety, through the body itself. Freud wrote that repressed material "returns in disguise"—the stroke after years of emotional suffocation, the ulcer after years of silence, the chronic insomnia of a wife who cannot speak her desire to leave.

Thus emotional indigestion is not a metaphor. It is a psychosomatic reality, rooted in repression, attachment gone awry, and the dissolution of the individual ego into roles and masks demanded by culture, family, or class.

- How wealth also traps people.
- High-class marriages and fear of losing lifestyle, respect, or social standing.
- Emotional indigestion as status maintenance.
- Both men and women trapped by class expectations.
- Beyond the stark realities of financial hardship, a distinct and often unacknowledged form of psychological distress, aptly termed "emotional indigestion," permeates the lives of the affluent. Far from being exempt, individuals of wealth frequently find themselves ensnared in a gilded cage, where their very prosperity becomes a source of significant internal conflict and suffering.
- This "indigestion" manifests as a profound inability to process and express genuine emotions, stemming from the immense pressures inherent in maintaining a lavish

lifestyle, societal standing, and generational expectations. High-class marriages, in particular, often serve as prime examples of this phenomenon. Marriages within affluent circles are frequently less about personal fulfillment and more about strategic alliances, solidifying wealth, power, or social connections. The fear of dissolving such a union extends far beyond mere heartbreak; it encompasses the terrifying prospect of losing not just a partner, but an entire lifestyle, professional network, and the crucial respect or social standing that underpins their identity. The potential for public scrutiny, reputational damage, and financial precarity (even for the wealthier party, due to asset division or public perception) creates an overwhelming incentive to maintain the facade of a perfect life, regardless of the underlying unhappiness.

- Consequently, emotional indigestion becomes a core component of status maintenance. Authentic feelings—whether of loneliness, resentment, unfulfillment, or even simple boredom—are rigorously suppressed to present an unblemished image of success and contentment. This constant performance, the need to uphold appearances for the sake of social capital, means that genuine human experiences are denied expression, festering internally and leading to chronic stress, anxiety, and a feeling of being perpetually unanchored. The stomach clenches, the mind races, but the lips must smile.
- Crucially, this trap of class expectations ensnares both men and women, albeit often through different, gendered pressures. Men in these echelons are frequently burdened by the expectation to be stoic providers, unwavering leaders, and the ultimate architects of financial empires, suppressing any vulnerability or doubt. They must navigate

a world of high-stakes business deals, managing immense wealth, and ensuring the continuity of family legacies, often at the cost of personal relationships or mental well-being. Women, on the other hand, are often expected to be the perfect socialites, the impeccable hostesses, the silent supporters of their husbands' careers, and the flawless embodiments of the family's prestige. They might be pressured to maintain a certain physical appearance, manage complex social calendars, or endure personal indignities for the sake of the family's reputation and financial stability. For both, the ultimate price of their privilege is often a profound isolation and the silent, corrosive weight of unacknowledged emotional pain—a pervasive emotional indigestion that wealth, paradoxically, only exacerbates.

Workbook Section: Reclaiming Selfhood

Reflection Questions

1. In my relationship(s), where have I dissolved into a role instead of living as myself?
2. What fears keep me bound—fear of poverty, fear of humiliation, fear of being alone?
3. Whom does my partner symbolize unconsciously? A parent, prestige, protection?

Small Step

Write down one quality or passion that belongs to you alone, independent of partner, family, or social standing. Commit to practicing it this week, even if for five minutes.

Affirmation

"I am more than my role, more than my fear. I reclaim the self that is mine."

Exercise

- Imagine yourself outside the relationship: What survives? Write a short paragraph about who you are when titles, wealth, or roles are stripped away.
- Seal it in an envelope labeled "My Self Beyond the Mask." Open it six months later to measure your growth.

Chapter 5: Men and Emotional Indigestion

Key Arguments

- Men struggle differently but deeply: they fear losing class identity tied to their wives or partners.
- Patriarchal expectations of masculinity prevent men from expressing emotional pain.
- Men may oppress women as a way to maintain their own fragile identities.

Examples

- A man who stays in a loveless marriage because leaving would signal weakness.
- A rural husband who mocks his wife but fears she might leave, because she represents his "manhood" in the community.

Therapists and Hidden Struggles

- Even therapists and mental health professionals are not immune.
- Many carry unresolved indigestions from their past or current relationships, which influence the way they help others.
- This cycle perpetuates unresolved pain across families, communities, and even the helping professions.

Therapists, often seen as paragons of mental well-being and emotional resilience, are in fact not immune to the very human struggles they help others navigate.

Even these dedicated mental health professionals, despite their extensive training and profound understanding of psychological principles, are fallible individuals who face life's adversities, personal traumas, and the complex dynamics of their own relationships. Like anyone else, they can experience burnout, grief, anxiety, depression, and the lingering effects of their past.

Crucially, many carry unresolved "indigestions" – deep-seated emotional pain, unaddressed traumas, or dysfunctional relational patterns – from their past or even current relationships. These unacknowledged or unhealed wounds, often stemming from family of origin issues, personal losses, or difficult romantic partnerships, do not simply vanish when they step into the therapeutic space. Instead, they can subtly, or sometimes overtly, influence the way they perceive, interpret, and ultimately help their clients. This can manifest as blind spots, unconscious biases, countertransference (projecting their own unresolved issues onto clients), empathy fatigue, or an inability to hold space for certain emotions or experiences that mirror their own unaddressed pain. The unspoken truth is that a therapist's internal landscape directly shapes the efficacy and safety of the therapeutic container they offer.

This precarious reality inevitably perpetuates a cycle of unresolved pain that ripples across families, communities, and disturbingly, even within the helping professions themselves. When therapists operate from a place of unaddressed wounds, they risk offering incomplete healing, reinforcing unhealthy patterns, or even inadvertently re-traumatizing vulnerable clients. This not only hinders individual progress but can erode trust in the therapeutic process itself, creating a systemic challenge where the very people meant to facilitate healing inadvertently contribute to the ongoing transmission of intergenerational emotional burdens. It underscores an urgent ethical imperative for therapists to engage in ongoing self-reflection, robust supervision, and their own personal therapy to ensure their "instrument" is finely tuned and free from obstructing static.

The profound implications of this overlap between personal and professional unresolved pain become particularly stark when examining the nexus of women, marriage, and profound dependency. This confluence presents an extraordinarily complex and often intractable challenge for therapeutic assistance, frequently manifesting as deep-seated emotional "indigestion" – a chronic state of psychological distress, suppressed rage, pervasive grief, and an erosion of self-identity that is exceptionally difficult to unravel and resolve.

For countless women, their circumstances are tragically defined by their entrapment in marital bonds they did not genuinely choose. This can stem from diverse and deeply systemic roots: arranged unions where personal consent is a secondary consideration to family honor, tradition, or economic alliance; marriages necessitated by sheer financial survival in contexts where a woman's economic viability outside of marriage is non-existent; or unions rigidly upheld by overwhelming cultural, religious, or societal expectations that brand divorce or singlehood as a source of indelible shame and ostracism. These external pressures often override personal desire, agency, and even physical safety, forcing women into profoundly disempowering situations.

The prospect of liberation from such suffocating arrangements becomes virtually impossible due to a glaring absence of fundamental support structures. Without access to education, viable employment opportunities, or robust social support networks, the material and social barriers to leaving are insurmountable.

The pervasive, paralyzing fear of destitution – of homelessness, starvation, losing custody of children, or becoming a social pariah – overwhelmingly outweighs the profound psychological and physical pain of remaining in an untenable marriage. This isn't merely a calculation of pain versus fear; it's a stark recognition of existential threat.

Furthermore, the seemingly simple option of returning "home" is frequently non-existent or equally unfeasible. For many, there literally is no safe or sustainable place to return to, often due to similar conditions of poverty, overcrowding, or even the risk of further abuse within their natal families or communities.

The burden of adding another mouth to feed, or the social stigma associated with a "failed" marriage, can render such a move impractical or undesirable for all involved. This lack of a viable escape route definitively cements their reliance on these often damaging marital structures, transforming what might otherwise be a temporary challenge into a life sentence of emotional duress. Consequently, any path to genuine emotional healing for these women becomes an incredibly slow, arduous, and deeply nuanced process, requiring not just individual therapy but often systemic shifts in societal support, economic empowerment, and cultural norms that are far beyond the scope of a typical therapeutic encounter.

Through a Freudian lens, the intricate tapestry of human relationships, particularly within the challenging socio-cultural contexts presented, reveals deep-seated unconscious dynamics centered on attachment, repression, transference, and the fragile state of the ego.

At the core, our earliest attachments – the primal libidinal bonds formed with primary caregivers – profoundly shape our adult relational patterns. When these foundational needs are unmet or fraught with anxiety, individuals develop complex defensive mechanisms to protect their nascent ego. For village women in arranged marriages, often stripped of agency, their emotional landscape might be dominated by a profound repression of personal desire, grief, or anger, forced underground by societal and familial superegoic dictates. Their attachments become pathways for the unconscious re-enactment of early experiences of powerlessness or conditional love, leading to a palpable sense of emotional truncation, where the ego's natural striving for self-actualization is stifled.

The struggles of educated professionals in Pretoria and men grappling with masculinity in North West offer a compelling illustration of these Freudian concepts. Men struggle differently but deeply, often fearing the perceived ego dissolution that would accompany a loss of class identity or social standing, particularly if tied to their wives or partners. This fear is not merely economic; it taps into a deeper, unconscious anxiety about self-worth and social castration.

The pervasive patriarchal expectations of masculinity function as a harsh superego, dictating that emotional pain, vulnerability, or failure are unacceptable. This societal pressure forces a profound repression of authentic feelings, pushing anxiety, fear, and sadness into the unconscious where they fester, manifesting as symptoms, anger, or rigid behaviors.

In this context, men may oppress women as a way to maintain their own fragile identities. This isn't a conscious, malicious act in all cases, but a desperate, unconscious defensive maneuver to prop up an ego constantly under siege by internal and external pressures.

The rural husband who mocks his wife but secretly fears her departure exemplifies this; her presence, even if derided, serves as an external validation of his "manhood" in the community, a crucial prop for his faltering ego. His mocking might be a form of transference, displacing his own insecurities or internalized criticisms onto her. Similarly, a man who stays in a loveless marriage, despite profound unhappiness, does so because leaving would signal "weakness" – a catastrophic blow to his ego's carefully constructed facade, threatening a symbolic death of his social self. His inability to articulate his pain or seek genuine connection reflects the extent of his repression, where vital emotional energy is bound up in maintaining appearances rather than resolving internal conflict.

Even therapists and mental health professionals are not immune to these deep-seated dynamics. As individuals, they also carry their own unresolved indigestions – their own unexamined attachment patterns, repressed traumas, and unacknowledged transference issues from past or current relationships. This personal emotional "baggage" can unconsciously influence their perceptions, interpretations, and even the therapeutic interventions they offer, creating blind spots or leading to counter-transference reactions that impede genuine healing. Without rigorous self-analysis and external supervision, this cycle perpetuates unresolved pain across families, communities, and tragically, even within the very helping professions designed to alleviate suffering, ensuring that the unconscious continues to exert its formidable power, shaping destinies beneath the surface of conscious awareness.

Case study

The city breathed an unending hum—a constant pulse of footsteps, distant sirens, and neon lights flickering against the night sky. In a modest office tucked between a bustling café and a boutique bookstore, Dr. Eleanor Chase sat behind her desk, her eyes tracing the worn edges of a notebook. She was a therapist, a beacon for those lost in the shadows of their minds. Yet tonight, a subtle weight pressed down on her shoulders, more suffocating than usual.

Across from her, Marcus shifted uncomfortably in his chair, eyes darting to the window before settling back on her. He was a frequent visitor, and like many in this city, carried a silent burden.

"You seem distant tonight," Eleanor observed gently.

"I guess I just... don't know how to start," Marcus admitted, voice low. "Sometimes, I think I'm just repeating the same mistakes, no matter how hard I try to fix things."

Eleanor nodded, her expression thoughtful. "It's often the unresolved things from our past that shape how we move through the present. Do you want to tell me what's been bothering you?"

He hesitated, then finally sighed. "My father was never really there. Always busy, always chasing something else. I think I've been trying to prove myself, to get his attention, even if he's not around anymore."

Eleanor's eyes softened. "That cycle—*highlighted—it's something many people carry. Even those who help others the most, like therapists, aren't immune. We all have our echoes, our hidden struggles."*

She paused, glancing at the city's glowing skyline beyond the window. "Sometimes, I wonder how much of my own pain influences how I guide my clients. It's like trying to help others with a mirror fogged by my own unresolved issues."

Marcus looked at her, surprised. "You seem so composed. I didn't realize..."

"We all wear masks," she said quietly. "Even in the helping professions, we're just as vulnerable. Our unresolved indigestions from the past—our own stories—affect the way we connect, the way we listen, the way we heal."

A silence settled between them, the city's hum washing over the room.

"So, what do we do with that?" Marcus finally asked.

Eleanor offered a faint smile. "We acknowledge it. We're human, after all. And maybe, understanding our own hidden struggles is the first step toward breaking the cycle. Because pain, if left unexamined, simply perpetuates—across families, communities, even within those who dedicate their lives to helping others."

Outside, the city thrummed on, unaware of the quiet battles happening behind closed doors—battles that echoed far beyond the therapy room, fueling a cycle of unresolved pain that refused to stay buried.

- Men's struggles: associating women with class, identity, and respect.
- Fear of starting over and societal pressure on masculinity.
- Hidden suffering of men who cannot detach.
- The concept of "emotional indigestion" perfectly encapsulates a profound and often unspoken struggle faced by many men, where unprocessed and unresolved emotional pain festers beneath the surface. This silent suffering is deeply rooted in several interconnected societal and personal pressures:
- For many men, the female partner becomes inextricably linked to their very sense of self-worth and societal standing. Men's struggles often revolve around associating

> women with their class, identity, and respect. A woman is not merely a companion but often a reflection of his success, his good taste, his ability to provide, and his social currency. Her perceived status, beauty, or accomplishments can elevate his own standing in the eyes of the world and, crucially, in his own estimation. Therefore, the breakdown of a relationship, or even just the fear of it, isn't just a loss of companionship; it's a direct assault on his identity, a potential demotion in his perceived class, and a profound blow to his sense of respect, both from others and for himself. This external validation becomes a heavy anchor, making detachment incredibly difficult.

This internal calculus is compounded by the daunting prospect of "starting over," which isn't just about finding a new partner, but dismantling an entire life structure—home, finances, social circles, and future plans. For men, this challenge is often exacerbated by societal pressure on masculinity, which rigidly dictates strength, stoicism, and unwavering competence.

The narrative for men often includes being the provider, the protector, the stable foundation. A relationship failure, particularly a perceived personal one, can feel like a profound failure of their core masculine identity. The fear of appearing weak, of admitting defeat, or of facing the immense practical and emotional upheaval of rebuilding from scratch, traps many men in situations they desperately want to escape. The weight of "what will others think?" or "Am I less of a man for this?" can be crushing.

Consequently, a silent, pervasive suffering takes root in men who cannot detach, even when a relationship is clearly detrimental. This emotional inability to let go isn't necessarily a sign of love, but rather a desperate clinging to the identity, perceived status, and stability that the relationship represents. This hidden suffering manifests not in overt expressions of grief, but in internalized pain, chronic stress, emotional numbness, or even destructive coping mechanisms like anger, isolation, or substance abuse.

This unseen torment is the essence of their emotional indigestion – a deep, unacknowledged wound that festers beneath a veneer of composure, leaving them emotionally constipated and profoundly unwell. They carry this heavy burden in private, unable or unwilling to articulate the complex interplay of lost identity, shattered external validation, and the terrifying prospect of starting anew, all under the unforgiving gaze of societal expectations of masculinity.

Reflection Questions

1. What pressures do I feel as a man/woman to "look strong" in relationships?
2. Do I hide my fears or pains to maintain an image?

Exercise

- Silent Truth Letter: Write a private letter to yourself about fears you've never admitted. You don't need to share it—just acknowledge your truth.

Part III: The Ripple Effects

Chapter 6: Therapists and Healers Are Not Exempt

Key Arguments

- Even mental health professionals carry unresolved indigestion.
- Helpers often unconsciously bring their own unresolved dependency issues into their practice.
- Healing requires therapists to confront their own indigestions.

Examples

- A therapist who counsels women to leave abusive marriages but remains in her own.
- A pastor giving marital advice while secretly trapped in emotional indigestion himself.

Breaking Free from Emotional Indigestion

- Healing requires courage to face the fear of starting over.
- Therapy must address:
    - Fear of change
    - Fear of going back to poverty or simplicity
    - Fear of losing status
    - Fear of being alone

- Psychoanalysis helps trace these fears back to childhood experiences of attachment, dependency, or abandonment.
- Nutritional and holistic perspectives remind us that the body also digests emotions—what we suppress eventually shows up in physical illness.

- Breaking Free from Emotional Indigestion: A Holistic Journey Towards Inner Liberation
- The metaphor of "emotional indigestion" perfectly encapsulates the profound discomfort and systemic distress that arises when we fail to process, acknowledge, and release the toxic residues of unaddressed feelings and experiences. It's a psychic burden, a persistent gnawing in the gut of our soul, signalling that our inner world is struggling to metabolize the difficult truths and unresolved conflicts of life. True healing from this state is not merely an intellectual exercise; it's a courageous and often daunting reclamation of self, demanding a comprehensive approach that addresses the mind, body, and spirit.

- At the heart of breaking free lies an undeniable truth: healing requires the sheer courage to face the fear of starting over. This isn't just about initiating a new chapter; it's about dismantling existing, often comfortable, structures – routines, relationships, even identities – that, despite their familiarity, have become prisons. It demands stepping into the vast, unknown territory of self-discovery, where old coping mechanisms no longer serve, and the contours of a new, healthier life are yet to be formed. This leap of faith, fraught with trepidation, is the first and most critical step towards genuine liberation.

- For this brave journey to be successful, therapy must delve deeply into the spectrum of fears that often paralyze us. These aren't superficial anxieties but deeply ingrained psychological barriers that protect the ego from perceived threats:
- Fear of Change: This isn't just a resistance to novelty, but a profound anxiety about disrupting established patterns, losing predictability, and relinquishing the illusion of

control. It's the fear that the unknown path, however promising, might be worse than the known discomfort.

- Fear of Going Back to Poverty or Simplicity: Beyond mere financial insecurity, this taps into a deep-seated scarcity mindset and a fear of losing perceived status or comfort. It's the anxiety that shedding excess emotional baggage might also mean stripping away the material or social markers that have become intertwined with one's sense of worth and security.

- Fear of Losing Status: Often rooted in ego identification and societal conditioning, this fear manifests as a desperate clinging to professional achievements, social standing, or external validation. It's the terror of being seen as less successful, less intelligent, or less significant, thereby threatening one's identity and sense of belonging within a chosen community.

- Fear of Being Alone: Perhaps the most primal of fears, this encompasses not just physical solitude but a profound existential dread of unworthiness, abandonment, and a lack of support. It's the terror of confronting one's inner landscape without the distraction or perceived safety net of others, revealing potential feelings of emptiness or inadequacy.

- To truly dismantle these formidable fears, psychoanalysis offers a powerful lens, helping to trace their intricate roots back to formative childhood experiences. This deep dive into the unconscious mind explores the early imprints of attachment, dependency, and abandonment dynamics. Through this process, individuals can begin to understand how their earliest interactions with caregivers shaped their core beliefs about relationships, safety, self-worth, and the world. Unresolved anxieties from a distant past – a perceived lack of secure attachment, overwhelming dependency needs, or the profound pain of childhood abandonment – often manifest as the very fears that hinder adult growth and perpetuates emotional indigestion. By bringing these unconscious patterns into conscious awareness, therapy provides the opportunity to re-parent the inner child and forge healthier emotional responses.

- Beyond the psychological realm, a crucial component of breaking free from emotional indigestion involves embracing nutritional and holistic perspectives, which profoundly remind us that the body also digests emotions. Life's experiences are not merely cerebral events; they are felt, absorbed, and processed on a cellular level. What we suppress – the anger we swallow, the grief we deny, the fear we refuse to acknowledge – does not simply vanish. Instead, it becomes internalized, creating energetic blockages, chronic stress responses, and systemic imbalances that eventually show up in tangible physical illness. From digestive issues like IBS and acid reflux to autoimmune disorders, chronic pain, and nervous system dysregulation, the body often becomes the silent canvas upon which our unexpressed emotions are painted. Holistic practices, including mindful eating, targeted nutrition, breathwork, and movement, coupled with emotional release techniques, provide pathways for the body to metabolize these suppressed feelings, restoring balance and paving the way for integrated, sustainable well-being.

- In essence, breaking free from emotional indigestion is a brave odyssey requiring a multi-faceted approach. It's a commitment to confront deeply entrenched fears, understand their historical roots, and honor the intricate connection between our emotional and physical health. Only through this integrated healing can we truly liberate ourselves, transforming an often painful internal struggle into a vibrant process of profound self-discovery and lasting peace

Case study

The city's hum was relentless that morning—cars honking, sirens wailing, the distant clatter of lives crowded together in a dance of chaos and hope. Mira sat on the balcony of her cramped apartment, clutching a steaming mug of coffee, her eyes fixated on the skyline that stretched endlessly. Yet beneath the city's vibrant pulse, she felt an ache—a gnawing sense of something unspoken, unresolved.

"It's like my emotions are stuck in traffic," she murmured to herself, swirling her coffee absently. "Too much to process, and nowhere for it to go."

Mira had always believed that healing was a matter of effort—therapy books, meditation, late-night talks with friends. But lately, she wondered if she was merely skimming the surface, avoiding the deeper fears that tethered her. The fear of change, the dread of losing her carefully built status, the haunting worry of ending up alone again—these shadows clung to her like a second skin.

She remembered her childhood in the nearby village, where simplicity was a shield and attachment was raw and visceral. Her mother's gentle voice echoed in her mind: "Change is dangerous, Mira. Stay safe, stay the same." But safety in sameness often felt like emotional indigestion—uncomfortable, persistent, and ultimately, harmful.

A knock at her door pulled her back. She opened it to find her neighbor, Raj, a thoughtful man whose calm demeanor belied his own battles.

"You look lost in thought," Raj observed softly.

"Just trying to breathe through everything," Mira admitted, stepping aside. "Sometimes I think I'm carrying around this heavy emotional baggage. It's like my body's trying to tell me something, but I don't know what."

Raj nodded knowingly. "I read somewhere that our bodies digest emotions just like food. If we suppress them, they don't just disappear—they turn into illness, into pain. Healing requires us to face the fears rooted deep in childhood—fear of abandonment, dependency, and losing what we hold dear."

Mira's eyes flickered with a newfound curiosity. "So, therapy isn't just about talking. It's about tracing these fears back to their roots, understanding where they come from?"

"Exactly. And sometimes, it takes courage—the courage to start over, to risk losing what we cling to. But in doing so, we make space for something healthier to grow."

She took a deep breath, feeling the weight of her fears pressing against her chest. "Maybe it's time I stop feeding my emotional indigestion and start digesting what's truly mine to heal."

As the city's morning scene unfurled beyond her window, Mira felt a flicker of hope—a whisper that breaking free from the cycle was possible, even in the chaos. All it took was the courage to face the fears, one step at a time.

Reflection Questions

1. Do I give advice to others that I don't follow myself?
2. Where in my own life am I carrying indigestion I ask others to release?

Exercise

- Mirror Practice: Write down one healing message you often give others. Then practice saying it aloud to yourself daily for one week.

- Fragile Identities: Men fear losing status or social recognition tied to their wives or partners.
- Patriarchal Suppression: Emotional expression is often repressed to maintain a façade of strength.
- Interpersonal Oppression: Emotional fragility can

translate into controlling or abusive behaviors.

Examples:

- A man remains in a loveless marriage because leaving would signify weakness in his community.
- A rural husband mocks his wife but secretly fears abandonment, tying his ego to her presence.

Therapists and Hidden Struggles:

Even trained mental health professionals carry unresolved emotional indigestions. Their capacity to help is influenced by their own repressed experiences, perpetuating cycles of unresolved pain across families and communities.

Emotional Indigestion Through Freud's Lens

Freud's psychoanalytic framework provides a powerful lens for understanding emotional indigestion, particularly in the ways unresolved attachment, repression, and transference shape our relational lives. Emotional indigestion often begins in early life, rooted in attachment patterns with caregivers, and manifests later in adult relationships as dependency, fear of separation, or compulsive relational behaviors.

Attachment and Dependency

Attachment theory, which Freud's work on early object relations complements, posits that the bonds we form in childhood create templates for adult intimacy. Men in New York may display compulsive workaholism to avoid vulnerability in relationships, while men in Gabon or Ghana may remain emotionally distant to maintain social or financial control. In Zimbabwe or Swaziland, the weight of patriarchal expectations often enforces emotional repression, while in Greece, the UK, and Australia, men might struggle with emotional expression despite liberal societal norms, fearing judgment or loss of status.

Village women, across African contexts or rural Europe, often endure a heightened dependency on male partners—whether for survival, social validation, or access to resources—mirroring the unconscious attachment patterns Freud described. These patterns reinforce emotional indigestion when they feel unable to separate their identity from the relational context.

Repression and Ego Dissolution

Repression—the unconscious blocking of unacceptable desires or painful memories—is central to emotional indigestion. A man in New York who experienced early abandonment may repress fear of intimacy, manifesting as emotional withdrawal from his partner. In Nigeria, a wealthy man may repress vulnerability, clinging to material symbols of control, while a woman in a village in Swaziland may repress resentment against an oppressive partner to avoid destabilizing her survival.

Ego dissolution occurs when a person loses a sense of self within a relationship. This is evident globally: men across Europe or Australia may struggle with identity in partnerships due to rigid societal roles, while women in African villages experience similar dissolution when survival and happiness are outsourced entirely to a partner. The "self" becomes indistinguishable from the relational "other," creating a fertile ground for emotional indigestion.

Transference in Relationships and Therapy

Transference, Freud's concept of redirecting feelings from one relationship onto another, is critical in understanding relational dynamics. Men and women unconsciously project unresolved childhood fears and desires onto partners, often perpetuating cycles of dependency and conflict. For instance:

- A therapist in London counseling women to leave abusive marriages may remain trapped in her own unhealthy relationship, unconsciously projecting her fears onto clients.
- A pastor in Zimbabwe giving marital guidance may struggle with his own unresolved dependency, subtly transmitting anxiety, fear of loss, or repression into his counsel.
- A healer in Ghana or a village in Gabon may advise others on emotional resilience while avoiding confrontation with their own fear of starting over, dependence, or loss of status.

These examples highlight that even those trained to guide others—therapists, pastors, healers—are not exempt from emotional indigestion. Their ability to help is intertwined with their willingness to confront their own unresolved attachments.

Breaking Free from Emotional Indigestion

Healing requires courage and intentionality. Psychoanalysis reveals that the fear underpinning emotional indigestion often traces back to childhood experiences of attachment, abandonment, and dependency. Therapy must address:

- Fear of change: anxiety about moving away from a familiar, even if unhealthy, relationship.
- Fear of going back to poverty or simplicity: common in low-income or resource-dependent contexts.
- Fear of losing status: particularly in high-income or socially stratified societies.
- Fear of being alone: an existential terror that echoes early attachment disruptions.

Additionally, Freud's framework reminds us that the body stores unprocessed emotions. Nutritional and holistic perspectives emphasize that emotional suppression manifests physically: high blood pressure, digestive disorders, chronic fatigue, and other somatic symptoms often accompany unresolved emotional indigestion.

Key Takeaways

- Emotional indigestion is universal; it transcends geography, culture, and socio-economic class.
- Men in New York, Australia, and Europe and village women in Zimbabwe, Ghana, and Gabon experience it differently, shaped by societal norms and attachment histories.
- Transference, repression, and ego dissolution perpetuate dependency cycles.
- Therapists, pastors, and healers must confront their own unresolved indigestion to authentically support others.
- Liberation requires facing fears—of change, of simplicity, of loss, and of solitude—while cultivating self-generated joy and autonomy.

Conclusion: Towards Emotional Freedom

- Emotional indigestion is a universal struggle, crossing boundaries of class, education, and profession.
- The way forward is not in clinging to relationships at any cost, but in rediscovering the self that exists outside of attachment.
- True healing comes when people learn to generate joy, stability, and meaning from within, rather than outsourcing these to their partners.

The city never truly slept, but sometimes, in its endless hum, you could forget to listen. Mara sat on her balcony, gazing out over the flickering skyline—neon signs blinking like distant stars, cars streaking by in hurried patterns. Yet beneath that vibrant chaos, a quiet ache gnawed at her, an emotional indigestion that nothing seemed to settle.

She had always believed that love—romance, partnership—was the ultimate remedy, the way to heal every ache. But lately, she wondered if she'd been feeding herself the wrong prescription. The more she clung to her relationship with Daniel, the more her heart felt like a balloon slowly losing air, stretched thin by expectations she couldn't fulfill.

Her phone buzzed on the table, and she saw his name. She hesitated, then answered. "Hey," she whispered, voice tentative.

"Hey," Daniel's voice was warm, but there was an edge of fatigue. "Are you coming over tonight?"

"I... I don't know, Daniel," she hesitated. "I've been thinking about us, about myself. I need to find where I end and we begin."

There was a pause on the other end. "You mean you're tired of trying?"

She looked out over the city again, a place that thrived on constant motion—yet she felt static, stuck in a cycle of giving and losing herself. "I think the way forward isn't in clinging to us at any cost," she finally said, voice trembling. "I need to rediscover who I am beyond us. Maybe, it's time I learned to generate joy, stability, and meaning from within, rather than outsourcing it to someone else."

The line was silent for a moment. Then Daniel sighed. "I want that for you, Mara. I just wish I knew how."

She pressed her forehead against the cool glass, feeling the city's pulse beneath her skin. This is a universal struggle— crossing boundaries of class, education, and profession. Whether in the bustling streets or in the quiet corners of a suburban street, emotional indigestion gnaws at everyone, no matter how successful or grounded they seem.

Mara closed her eyes, envisioning a different life. One where she could stand on her own, rooted in herself, capable of generating her own joy. A life where healing was no longer a borrowed emotion but a cultivated strength from within.

Because true healing, she understood now, comes when people learn to generate joy, stability, and meaning from within, rather than depending on others to fill the void. Her journey would begin here, in the city's chaos and quiet, to find the quiet resilience lying beneath the surface.

And as the city's lights flickered in the darkness, Mara felt a faint hope stir—a whisper that she was finally ready to embrace herself, beyond attachment, beyond the ache.

Emotional Indigestion – Escaping Dependency in Relationships

Introduction: Naming the Silent Struggle

- Define emotional indigestion as the inability to move on, detach, or rediscover oneself outside of a relationship.
- Why this concept matters: the silent epidemic across rural, urban, and even professional spaces.
- State the purpose of the book: to explore the roots, effects, and healing paths of emotional indigestion.
- Personal and community observations as entry point (villages, health struggles, marriages, poverty).

Naming the Silent Struggle

Imagine a meal that just won't digest. It sits heavy, causing discomfort, bloat, and a lingering sense of unease long after the plate has been cleared. This physical analogy offers a potent glimpse into "emotional indigestion" – a profoundly debilitating, yet often unacknowledged, state of being. At its core, emotional indigestion is the persistent inability to move on, to truly detach, or to fully rediscover and reclaim one's own identity and sense of self outside the context of a significant relationship, whether it has ended, transformed, or remains deeply dysfunctional. It's the sensation of a past relationship, or a current unhealthy dynamic, being perpetually "stuck" within one's emotional system, preventing new growth and perpetuating a cycle of internal discomfort.

This isn't merely a fleeting phase of heartache; it's a chronic spiritual and psychological stagnation that has profound implications. It matters immensely because emotional indigestion has quietly metastasized into a silent epidemic, afflicting countless individuals across every demographic and societal stratum. From the bustling anonymity of urban centers to the close-knit communities of rural villages, and even within the seemingly composed corridors of professional life, countless individuals suffer in silence. They wear brave faces, fulfilling duties and roles, while internally grappling with the undigested residues of past or present relational dynamics, holding them captive in a cycle of dependency and self-erasure. Its insidious nature lies in its often-invisible symptoms, manifesting as chronic anxiety, unexplained fatigue, persistent low self-esteem, or a pervasive sense of being incomplete without another person – all while the world expects a quick "get over it."

This book aims to shine a much-needed light into this hidden struggle. Our purpose is not merely to name this pervasive condition but to embark on a comprehensive journey of understanding. We will meticulously explore the multifaceted roots of emotional indigestion – delving into childhood patterns, societal pressures, cultural norms, and the insidious nature of codependency.

We will examine its far-reaching effects on mental health, physical well-being, personal growth, and future relationships, revealing how deeply this condition can permeate every aspect of one's life. Most crucially, however, we will chart accessible, compassionate, and practical healing paths, offering guidance on how to process these undigested experiences, cultivate genuine self-reliance, reclaim personal agency, and ultimately, rediscover the vibrant, autonomous self that lies buried beneath layers of relational dependency.

The genesis of this concept didn't emerge from abstract theory but from years of deeply personal and communal observation. It began in the heart of our villages, witnessing firsthand the quiet despair etched on faces, the unspoken grief that seemed to linger in the air long after a marriage dissolved or a loved one departed. It became evident in the startling correlation between persistent, unexplained health struggles and entangled emotional states, where the body seemed to manifest the very stagnation the soul endured.

I observed countless marriages, outwardly stable, yet inwardly decaying, held together not by genuine connection but by a crippling fear of independence, trapping individuals in a cycle of unfulfillment. Even the pervasive grip of poverty often seemed inextricably linked, not just to economic circumstances, but to a deeply ingrained emotional inability to break free from cycles of generational dependency and learned helplessness. These lived experiences – the hushed conversations, the tearful confessions, the quiet acts of resilience and despair – served as the crucible in which the concept of emotional indigestion was forged.

This book is, in essence, an empathetic response to those untold stories, a guide forged in the crucible of shared human experience, offering a roadmap out of the stuckness and into a future of profound personal liberation.

Part IV: The Ripple Effects

- The irony of helpers carrying unresolved indigestions.
- How unprocessed personal struggles affect therapy outcomes.
- The need for therapists to heal themselves.

Therapists and Healers Are Not Exempt

The irony of helpers carrying unresolved indigestions:

It is often assumed that therapists and healers are immune to emotional struggles and personal problems. However, the reality is that they are human beings too, with their own unique set of experiences, traumas, and challenges. In fact, therapists and healers may carry unresolved emotional indigestions from their past, which can impact their ability to effectively help their clients. This irony highlights the importance of self-awareness and personal growth in the field of therapy and healing.

How unprocessed personal struggles affect therapy outcomes:

When therapists and healers have unprocessed personal struggles, it can unintentionally affect their interactions with clients. For example, a therapist who has not dealt with their own anger issues may unknowingly project their feelings onto a client who is struggling with anger management. This can lead to misdiagnosis, ineffective treatment plans, and poor therapy outcomes. Furthermore, clients may sense the therapist's unresolved issues and feel less trusting or comfortable in the therapeutic relationship.

The need for therapists to heal themselves:

In order to provide effective and compassionate care to their clients, therapists and healers must prioritize their own healing and personal growth. This involves engaging in their own therapy, attending workshops and seminars, and seeking support from colleagues and mentors. By addressing their own emotional struggles, therapists can become more empathetic, insightful, and skilled in their work. Moreover, they can serve as positive role models for their clients, demonstrating the importance of self-care and personal growth in the healing process.

Therapists and healers are not exempt from the emotional struggles and personal challenges that affect us all. By acknowledging and addressing their own unresolved issues, therapists can improve the quality of their work and better support their clients on their healing journeys.

Chapter 7: Communities in Pain

Key Arguments

- Emotional indigestion is not just personal—it's a public health problem.
- Stress contributes to disease burdens in poor communities.
- Emotional suffering becomes intergenerational when parents pass down dependency models.
- Silence and stigma stop people from seeking help.

Examples

- A village where multiple women are sick, not from "witchcraft" but from unspoken relationship pain.
- Young girls raised to believe they cannot survive without a man, inheriting indigestion from their mothers

- Emotional indigestion as a public health issue.
- Epidemiological perspective: stress as a determinant of disease.
- Collective indigestion in villages: silence, stigma, and suppression.
- Emotional indigestion as intergenerational inheritance.

The concept of "Communities in Pain" delves into the profound, often unacknowledged suffering that permeates collective social structures, extending far beyond individual distress. It highlights how emotional wounds, when left unaddressed on a societal level, can manifest as widespread public health crises, impacting well-being, social cohesion, and future generations.

Emotional Indigestion as a Public Health Issue

Just as the body struggles to digest certain foods, leading to physical discomfort and illness, "emotional indigestion" refers to the inability of individuals and, by extension, communities to process, articulate, and resolve collective emotional burdens. This isn't merely a personal struggle; it's a societal malady. When large segments of a population are perpetually exposed to stressors such as poverty, systemic injustice, environmental degradation, or historical trauma, and lack the communal mechanisms for coping and healing, these unprocessed emotions fester. The chronic accumulation of fear, grief, anger, frustration, and helplessness can manifest as rising rates of mental health disorders (depression, anxiety, PTSD), substance abuse, domestic violence, social fragmentation, and even physical ailments. From a public health perspective, this "indigestion" drains resources, reduces productivity, erodes social capital, and necessitates proactive, community-wide interventions akin to addressing an infectious disease outbreak, focusing on resilience-building, psycho-social support, and trauma-informed care.

1. Epidemiological Perspective: Stress as a Determinant of Disease

Epidemiology, the study of the patterns, causes, and effects of health and disease conditions in defined populations, offers a crucial lens through which to understand community pain. From this perspective, chronic and pervasive stress is not just a psychological state but a potent determinant of both physical and mental disease. Prolonged exposure to stressors within a community—be it economic instability, political unrest, natural disasters, or discrimination—activates the body's fight-or-flight response, leading to sustained elevated cortisol levels, inflammation, and weakened immune systems. Epidemiological studies can track the correlation between communities experiencing high levels of collective stress and higher incidences of cardiovascular disease, diabetes, autoimmune disorders, chronic pain syndromes, and various mental illnesses. This perspective underscores that "pain" in communities is not abstract; it translates into quantifiable health outcomes, underscoring the urgent need for population-level interventions that address the root causes of stress and build community-wide coping capacities.

2. Collective Indigestion in Villages: Silence, Stigma, and Suppression

In many traditional or closely-knit communities, particularly in rural villages, the dynamics of emotional indigestion are exacerbated by deeply entrenched cultural norms.

A prevailing culture of silence often dictates that personal struggles, especially those related to mental health or emotional distress, are to be kept private, not shared, and certainly not aired publicly. This silence is frequently reinforced by stigma, where admitting vulnerability or seeking help for emotional pain is equated with weakness, shame, or even moral failing, bringing dishonor upon oneself or one's family. Consequently, there is widespread suppression of feelings.

Grief is endured in solitude, anger festers beneath polite exteriors, and anxiety is dismissed as a personal burden to be carried alone. This collective suppression prevents genuine dialogue, impedes the formation of support networks, and denies individuals access to necessary resources, leading to a silent epidemic of suffering that can manifest as unexplained physical ailments, increased aggression or apathy within families, or a general sense of communal stagnation and despair.

3. Emotional Indigestion as Intergenerational Inheritance

Perhaps most tragically, the unaddressed emotional indigestion within a community can become an insidious, intergenerational inheritance. Trauma, whether from war, famine, systemic oppression, or chronic poverty, when not collectively processed and healed, doesn't simply disappear with the passing of a generation. Instead, the coping mechanisms (or lack thereof), belief systems, and emotional patterns of the traumatized generation are subtly or overtly passed down.

Children raised in environments where emotions are suppressed, where communication is indirect, or where trust is eroded, learn these patterns themselves. They may inherit a predisposition to anxiety, depression, or difficulty forming healthy attachments, not through genetics, but through learned behaviors and the lingering psychological residue of unresolved collective pain. This creates cycles of suffering, where the "indigestion" of the past manifests as present-day challenges in family dynamics, community relations, and individual well-being, making it harder for future generations to thrive without targeted interventions that acknowledge and address these deep-seated historical wounds.

Reflection Questions

1. How does silence about emotional pain show up in my family or community?
2. What messages about dependency did I inherit from parents or culture?

Exercise

- Generational Reflection: Write down 3 beliefs about relationships you heard growing up (e.g., "A woman must stay no matter what"). Then rewrite them into healthier alternatives (e.g., "A woman deserves peace, safety, and freedom").

Emotional indigestion is often misconstrued as a purely individual phenomenon—a private struggle confined to the interiority of the mind. Yet when we consider the psychoanalytic framework, particularly Freud's notion of the unconscious, it becomes evident that these struggles are not merely personal but profoundly social. The unconscious does not operate in isolation; it is shaped by culture, society, and the relational environments in which we develop.

Communities, particularly those grappling with poverty, patriarchy, and intergenerational dependency, carry emotional indigestion collectively. The repression of feelings, the silence around relational suffering, and the habitual outsourcing of emotional well-being to others become public health issues, subtly shaping morbidity and mortality across generations.

Emotional Indigestion as Public Health

Freud emphasizes that unresolved conflicts in the unconscious manifest in conscious behavior, physical symptoms, and interpersonal patterns. In a rural village, for example, we often observe multiple women suffering not from witchcraft, as is culturally assumed, but from deep, unspoken relational pain. These women, trapped in marriages or partnerships defined by dependency, social expectation, or economic survival, embody Freud's concept of the return of the repressed: their unresolved fears and suppressed desires surface as chronic stress, hypertension, digestive disorders, and even somatic illness.

The psychological pain they endure is internalized, yet its effects ripple outward, shaping families, relationships, and ultimately the health of the community.

Carl Jung complements this perspective with his concept of the collective unconscious, suggesting that communities inherit patterns of thought, behavior, and relational expectations. Young girls raised in these villages, observing mothers who silently endure harmful or unsatisfying relationships, internalize these models as normative.

The unconscious message is clear: survival is contingent upon male approval, happiness is derived externally, and individual desire is secondary. These inherited patterns constitute what we may term intergenerational emotional indigestion, where the suffering of one generation becomes embedded in the next, perpetuating cycles of dependency, fear, and repression.

The Epidemiology of Stress

From a public health perspective, emotional indigestion can be understood as a determinant of disease. Chronic stress, rooted in unresolved relational dependency, activates physiological pathways that contribute to hypertension, strokes, diabetes, and other stress-related illnesses.

The villagers' unacknowledged emotional pain becomes a silent epidemic: the community manifests symptoms not through direct contagion but through shared emotional repression. Freud would interpret this as a collective neurosis, while Jung might identify the archetypal patterns of fear, subservience, and the shadow self, perpetuated unconsciously across households.

The role of silence and stigma cannot be overstated. Communities in which discussing relational dissatisfaction, marital conflict, or emotional dependency is taboo create fertile ground for chronic emotional indigestion. Here, repression is not merely internal—it is socially sanctioned. Women cannot express dissatisfaction for fear of social censure; men suppress vulnerability to maintain status. Over time, these patterns ossify, embedding dependency and emotional suppression as communal norms.

Intergenerational Inheritance

Consider a young girl growing up in a village in Zimbabwe or Ghana. She observes her mother, who has endured decades of emotional dependency, suppressed anger, and relational fear. Freud would argue that the girl internalizes the mother's unresolved conflicts, while Jung would recognize the transference of unconscious archetypes: the belief that survival and worth are contingent upon alignment with patriarchal structures. The girl's emerging psyche absorbs these patterns, predisposing her to the same emotional indigestion that afflicted her mother. The cycle is self-perpetuating: mothers, constrained by poverty and social norms, unconsciously model repression, while daughters inherit these patterns and normalize relational dependency. Emotional suffering thus becomes a form of inherited trauma, inscribed in the psyche long before the girl reaches adulthood.

Traditional Healing and the Church as Intervention

In many African villages, traditional healing and church-based interventions offer culturally accepted pathways to confront emotional indigestion. Freud's psychoanalysis emphasizes bringing unconscious material into consciousness to resolve internal conflict; Jung stresses individuation, integrating shadow aspects of the self. Traditional healers and church ministers, though sometimes operating outside formal psychological training, facilitate similar processes: confession, communal discussion, ritual, and symbolic acts create spaces where the repressed can emerge safely.

A village pastor may encourage women to recount the pains of marital life during counseling or prayer circles, allowing the community to witness the emotional reality previously silenced. Traditional healers may employ herbal remedies or rituals not merely for physical ailments but to symbolically process suppressed anger, fear, and grief. These practices, though culturally distinct from Western psychotherapy, address the psycho-emotional dimensions of indigestion, facilitating the release of long-repressed relational pain.

However, even these helpers are not immune to emotional indigestion themselves. Freud would caution that transference occurs in reverse: a healer who has unresolved dependency may unconsciously project fear, anxiety, or judgment onto the people they serve. Jung would observe that the healer or pastor often confronts their own shadow during these processes. The ethical and therapeutic imperative, therefore, is dual: communities must confront collective indigestion, and helpers must engage in self-analysis and individuation, ensuring their own unresolved conflicts do not perpetuate the cycle.

Collective Indigestion and Public Health Implications

The phenomenon of collective emotional indigestion has profound implications for public health. Chronic stress, unprocessed grief, and intergenerational trauma amplify disease burdens in resource-limited communities. Women and men endure repeated cycles of dependency, repression, and psychosomatic manifestations. Silence and stigma prevent access to formal mental health care, exacerbating the risk of chronic disease.

Recognizing emotional indigestion as both a personal and communal health concern is essential for developing interventions that honor cultural context while addressing psychological, social, and physiological dimensions.

Through the combined lens of Freud and Jung, emotional indigestion emerges as a multifaceted phenomenon—psychological, somatic, and social. The unconscious perpetuates patterns of dependency and repression, while intergenerational inheritance ensures that emotional suffering does not remain confined to a single individual.

Communities in pain require culturally sensitive interventions, incorporating therapy, pastoral guidance, and traditional healing practices to create spaces where the repressed can emerge safely. Only by acknowledging the unconscious, confronting the shadow, and processing collective repression can emotional indigestion be alleviated, reducing its profound public health consequences.

Global Essays of Emotional Indigestion

Emotional indigestion is universal, yet its manifestation differs according to cultural, social, and economic contexts. Using Freud's lens of the unconscious, repression, and transference, alongside Jung's insights into the collective unconscious and archetypes, we can trace how dependency, fear, and relational suffering shape lives across continents.

1. Men in New York, USA: The Anxiety of Independence

Jacob, a 38-year-old financial analyst in Manhattan, is constantly striving to succeed at work. Freud would argue that his compulsion is a displacement of repressed childhood fears: abandonment by a distant father left Jacob dependent on external validation. He fears intimacy with his partner, yet simultaneously craves connection—a paradox creating emotional indigestion.

Jung would interpret Jacob's situation as a struggle with the shadow self: the parts of himself he represses (vulnerability, dependence, need for affection) manifest as overwork, irritability, and relational withdrawal. Though he attends therapy weekly, he projects his anxieties onto his therapist (transference), unconsciously testing whether she can "hold" his unresolved fears, while remaining incapable of confronting the root of his dependency.

2. Men in Lagos, Nigeria: Status, Pride, and Repression

Emeka, a 42-year-old businessman, has a culturally sanctioned fear of appearing weak. Freud's theory suggests that repression of vulnerability is reinforced by social norms. Emotional indigestion manifests as chronic hypertension and insomnia. Emeka cannot acknowledge fear or sadness in front of his wife, lest he lose status.

In Jungian terms, the collective unconscious of Nigerian patriarchal society feeds an archetype of the invincible provider. Emotional expression is suppressed, and transference occurs when Emeka unconsciously expects subservience or admiration from his partner, mirroring unresolved childhood dependency needs.

3. Men in Europe (Greece, United Kingdom, Australia): Societal Expectations vs. Inner Longing

In Athens, Dimitris, 35, struggles with a professional life he finds unfulfilling but fears leaving due to societal expectation. Freud would highlight his repression of authentic desires—travel, artistry, emotional closeness—creating psychosomatic symptoms such as gastritis and chronic fatigue.

Across the UK and Australia, men like Thomas and Luke experience similar patterns: career success and social status mask deep anxiety about emotional dependency. Jung might see this as a confrontation with the anima, the inner feminine self that society teaches men to ignore. Failure to integrate this aspect results in relational tension, dependence on partners for emotional fulfillment, and prolonged emotional indigestion.

4. Village Women in Zimbabwe, Swaziland, Gabon, Ghana: Survival and Dependency

In a village outside Harare, Nomsa, a 28-year-old mother, endures an unhappy arranged marriage. Her dependency is not only emotional but economic: without her husband, she fears poverty and social ostracism. Freud's notion of repression explains how she suppresses anger and grief, resulting in chronic stress, hypertension, and recurring headaches.

Jung would highlight the role of the collective unconscious, noting that Nomsa's inherited maternal archetypes model silent endurance and dependency. Her mother and grandmother exhibited similar behaviors, creating a lineage of intergenerational emotional indigestion. Traditional healing practices and church gatherings offer Nomsa symbolic spaces to voice these repressed emotions—rituals and prayer serve as culturally sanctioned methods of catharsis.

5. Therapists and Healers: Not Exempt

Even professionals are vulnerable. A licensed therapist in London, counseling women on leaving abusive relationships, remains trapped in her own emotionally suffocating marriage. Freud would identify transference at play: she unconsciously projects her dependency anxieties onto her clients, guiding them in ways that reflect her unresolved fears.

Similarly, a pastor in a village in Gabon may counsel couples daily while struggling with his own emotional repression. Jung would see him confronting his shadow each day: the suppressed fear, dependency, and desire he cannot admit. Only by confronting their own emotional indigestions can these helpers authentically guide others.

6. The Role of Traditional Healing and Therapy

Across all contexts, culturally grounded interventions—whether therapy, pastoral guidance, or traditional healing—can facilitate the processing of repressed emotions. Rituals, storytelling, prayer, and psychoanalytic work allow communities to confront dependency, fear, and repression safely.

- In New York, Jacob's therapy involves dream analysis and guided introspection to integrate his shadow self.
- In Lagos, Emeka participates in counseling that combines cognitive-behavioral techniques with cultural rituals to acknowledge vulnerability.
- In Zimbabwe, Nomsa participates in church-based support circles, where confession and communal validation help release long-suppressed anger and fear.

Global Casebook of Emotional Indigestion

Emotional indigestion manifests universally, yet the ways it appears are shaped by cultural, economic, and social factors. Using Freud's lens of the unconscious, repression, and transference, along with Jung's insights into the collective unconscious and archetypes, we explore twelve vignettes illustrating how dependency, fear, and relational suffering traverse the globe. These cases highlight both personal struggles and communal dimensions, showing the interplay between psychology, physical health, and cultural healing practices.

1. Jacob – New York, USA

Jacob, 38, a financial analyst, overworks compulsively. Freud would identify this as displacement: early abandonment by his father left Jacob dependent on external validation. He fears intimacy, yet craves connection, creating chronic anxiety and digestive complaints—a physical manifestation of emotional indigestion. Jung would describe his shadow as the repressed need for vulnerability and emotional closeness. Therapy sessions reveal transference: he unconsciously tests whether his therapist can "contain" his unresolved fears.

Healing Approach

Psychoanalytic therapy with dream analysis and shadow integration. Support groups offer relational modeling.

2. Emeka – Lagos, Nigeria

Emeka, 42, a businessman, suppresses vulnerability to maintain status. Freud would link this repression to childhood experiences of dependency shame. Chronic stress manifests physically as hypertension and insomnia. Jung emphasizes the archetype of the invincible provider, ingrained in Nigeria's collective unconscious.

Healing Approach: Integrating culturally sensitive counseling, rituals acknowledging vulnerability, and family therapy to model healthy emotional expression.

3. Dimitris – Athens, Greece

Dimitris, 35, is trapped in a career that fulfills societal expectations but represses personal desire. Freud identifies his repression of authentic desires—artistic and relational—as the source of psychosomatic complaints. Jung would point to his struggle with the anima: the suppressed emotional, creative, and relational side of his psyche.

Healing Approach

Psychoanalytic therapy with focus on creative expression; community workshops for men to explore suppressed emotions safely.

4. Thomas – London, UK

Thomas, 40, is married with children, but emotional intimacy is absent. Freud sees projection and transference: he expects his partner to resolve childhood fears. Jung would interpret his inability to integrate the shadow self as creating persistent dissatisfaction.

Healing Approach

Psychoanalytic therapy combined with mindfulness and journaling to access and process repressed emotions.

5. Luke – Sydney, Australia

Luke, 36, hides emotional neediness to align with cultural norms of masculine independence. Freud links his repression to paternal abandonment. Jung notes that ignoring the anima prevents individuation. Chronic fatigue and stress-related illnesses mirror emotional indigestion.

Healing Approach: Therapy focusing on emotional literacy, shadow work, and support circles emphasizing emotional sharing among men.

6. Nomsa – Harare, Zimbabwe

Nomsa, 28, is trapped in an arranged marriage. Dependency is emotional and economic. Freud would identify her repression of anger and grief. Jung would highlight inherited archetypes of endurance and silence. Physical symptoms include hypertension and chronic pain.

Healing Approach: Church-based support circles and rituals allow safe expression of suppressed emotions; counseling addresses dependency and self-efficacy.

7. Amina – Accra, Ghana

Amina, 32, internalizes maternal messages that survival requires male approval. Freud interprets her compulsive caregiving as an unconscious repetition of childhood dependency patterns. Jung identifies archetypes of the nurturing yet silent mother shaping intergenerational indigestion.

Healing Approach: Psychoeducation on autonomy, empowerment programs, and traditional ritual interventions to symbolically release suppressed anger.

8. Fatima – Gabonese Village

Fatima, 40, experiences chronic stress from marital subjugation. Freud links her digestive and hypertensive complaints to repression of autonomy. Jung notes collective unconscious influences, perpetuating intergenerational fear of independence.

Healing Approach: Traditional healing combined with communal storytelling; herbal and ritual therapies symbolically support emotional release.

9. Elias – Johannesburg, South Africa

Elias, 45, a teacher, suffers anxiety from social expectations of masculinity. Freud sees unresolved dependency on parental approval as root cause. Jung emphasizes the shadow: repressed empathy and vulnerability.

Healing Approach: Psychoanalytic therapy and community men's groups to normalize emotional expression.

10. Sofia – Rural Italy

Sofia, 50, remains in a marriage out of social obligation. Freud highlights repression of desire and resentment. Jung identifies the archetype of the dutiful spouse perpetuating familial emotional indigestion.

Healing Approach: Individual therapy, expressive arts, and small peer groups to process unvoiced emotions.

11. Pastor Jean – Gabon

Pastor Jean advises couples daily yet struggles with his own unresolved relational fear. Freud identifies transference in his interactions with parishioners, reflecting unresolved unconscious fears. Jung sees confrontation with the shadow: the suppressed fear of loneliness and inadequacy.

Healing Approach: Psychoanalytic supervision, reflection, and shadow integration practices, combined with ritual and prayer as symbolic processing.

12. Therapist Helen – London, UK

Helen counsels women to leave abusive relationships while remaining in her own. Freud highlights transference and repression; Jung emphasizes the necessity of individuation for authentic guidance.

Healing Approach: Supervision, personal therapy, and shadow work; integrating psychoanalytic insight into clinical practice.

Part V: Breaking Free

Chapter 8: The Fear of Going Back

Key Arguments

- Fear of poverty, loneliness, and change.
- Why starting over feels like death.
- Emotional indigestion as fear of returning to "where I came from."
- Fear is the strongest chain: fear of poverty, loneliness, change, and shame.
- People choose to suffer rather than "go backwards."
- The hardest step in healing is facing the fear of starting over.

Examples

- A wealthy woman who stays in an abusive home because "going back to my old life would kill me."
- A rural wife who stays because "my parents are gone, and there's no bed for me in my old house."

Emotional indigestion is a remarkably intricate psychological phenomenon, far more complicated than a mere temporary discomfort, and it demands profound understanding for true emotional well-being and personal growth. Unlike physical indigestion, which often stems from dietary choices, its emotional counterpart arises from a complex stew of unresolved feelings, suppressed traumas, unaddressed anxieties, and the inability to process challenging life experiences. It manifests not just as a vague sense of unease, but as a persistent churning in one's inner landscape, leading to symptoms like anxiety, irritability, depression, a feeling of being stuck, or even physical ailments such as chronic fatigue or digestive issues. To truly navigate life with resilience and authenticity, one must delve into the roots of this internal disquiet, identifying the specific ingredients contributing to the emotional blockage.

One particularly potent and often overlooked source of this emotional turmoil is The Fear of Going Back. This isn't just a simple preference for progress; it's a deep-seated, often primal dread of regressing to a past state, a previous version of oneself, or a set of circumstances that were once painful or limiting.

This fear frequently crystallizes around very tangible anxieties:

Fear of poverty, loneliness, and change

The specter of poverty, whether financial or a general lack of resources and opportunity, is a powerful motivator. Having experienced scarcity, or witnessing it, the thought of returning to that state can be paralyzing. Similarly, the fear of loneliness—of losing one's current social connections, support systems, and the hard-won sense of belonging—can be terrifying. And underlying both is the fundamental human resistance to change, especially unpredictable, disruptive change.

The comfort of the known, however imperfect, often outweighs the daunting prospect of a complete upheaval, which necessitates starting from square one. This triad of fears represents a profound threat to an individual's sense of security, connection, and identity.

One particularly potent and often overlooked source of emotional turmoil is The Fear of Going Back. This isn't merely a preference for progress; it's a deep-seated, often primal dread of regressing to a past state, a previous version of oneself, or a set of circumstances that were once painful, limiting, or profoundly undesirable.

This fear frequently crystallizes around very tangible anxieties, often manifesting as:

The Fear of Scarcity and Want

The specter of poverty, whether financial or a general lack of resources and opportunity, is a powerful deterrent. Having experienced scarcity firsthand, or witnessed its devastating effects, the thought of returning to that state can be utterly paralyzing. It's a dread of losing hard-won stability and facing deprivation anew.

The Fear of Isolation and Loss of Connection

The thought of loneliness—of losing one's current social connections, vital support systems, and the hard-won sense of belonging—can be terrifying. This isn't just about being alone, but about the profound emotional void left by the absence of community and affirmation, a return to a state of unsupported vulnerability.

The Fear of Disruptive Change and Starting Over

Underlying these specific anxieties is the fundamental human resistance to change, especially unpredictable, disruptive change. The comfort of the known, however imperfect, often outweighs the daunting prospect of a complete upheaval that necessitates starting from square one. This fear is rooted in a deep-seated aversion to losing control, facing the unknown, and having to rebuild one's life from scratch.

Collectively, this triad of fears represents a profound threat to an individual's sense of security, connection, and identity, driving many decisions and anxieties.

Why starting over feels like death: For many, the idea of "starting over" isn't merely inconvenient; it carries the weight of a symbolic death. It implies the demise of an old identity, the obliteration of investments (time, effort, emotion) made in a particular path, and the loss of a future that was carefully envisioned. It can feel like an admission of failure, a dismantling of one's constructed self, and a return to a vulnerable, undefined state. This psychological "ego death" can be as terrifying as physical death, as it entails the complete unknown, the shedding of carefully built defenses, and the confrontation with a void where a clearly defined self used to be. The mourning for what was, or what could have been, settles deep in the emotional core, generating intense indigestion.

Emotional indigestion as fear of returning to "where I came from": This is perhaps the most visceral manifestation of this fear. "Where I came from" isn't just a geographical location; it's a loaded concept encompassing past struggles, limitations, traumas, or a certain level of existence that one fought tooth and nail to escape. It could be a place of emotional neglect, financial hardship, a toxic relationship dynamic, a limiting belief system, or a state of profound unhappiness. The thought of losing progress, of having all one's efforts undone, and being forced back into that original, undesirable "place" — whether literally or symbolically — creates an overwhelming sense of dread.

This fear curdles into emotional indigestion, manifesting as a pit in the stomach, a churning anxiety, a feeling of being trapped, or a deep, unyielding reluctance to move forward in any direction that even remotely resembles the path back.

Understanding this specific dread is crucial to processing the deeper layers of emotional indigestion, allowing individuals to address the roots of their avoidance and reclaim their forward momentum.

Reflection Questions

1. What is my biggest fear if I leave this relationship?
2. Is this fear based on reality or on what others will think of me?

Exercise

- Fear Ladder: List your fears about leaving (e.g., poverty, shame, loneliness). Rank them from most to least scary. For the lowest-ranked fear, brainstorm one step you could take to reduce it.

Chapter 9: Healing Pathways

Key Arguments

- Healing is possible but requires courage.
- Therapies: psychoanalysis (tracing back to childhood attachments), cognitive reframing, narrative healing, support groups.
- Holistic approaches: recognizing the link between mind and body (nutrition, exercise, stress management).
- Practical steps: rediscovering hobbies, practicing independence, creating small joys.
- Practical steps: self-recognition, boundary setting, reclaiming joy.
- Nutritional/holistic approaches: how emotions affect the body.
- Case examples of healing and transformation.

Examples

- A widow who learned to farm and found independence.
- A woman who began journaling, reclaiming her forgotten voicc.
- A man who left an unhealthy relationship and learned to cook for himself, symbolizing self-reliance.

- Healing Pathways: A Journey Towards Wholeness

The journey of healing is a profound and deeply personal odyssey, often requiring a multi-faceted approach to address the intricate interplay of mind, body, and spirit. "Healing Pathways" represents a comprehensive framework, integrating therapeutic insights, holistic wisdom, and practical steps to guide individuals toward profound transformation and sustained well-being.

- Therapy Approaches: Unlocking the Mind's Potential

At the heart of many healing journeys lies the exploration and understanding of one's inner landscape, facilitated by various therapeutic modalities:

- Psychoanalysis

    This deep-dive approach delves into the unconscious mind, seeking to uncover unresolved conflicts, repressed emotions, and early life experiences that may be shaping current behaviors and emotional patterns. Through a long-term, intensive process, individuals gain profound insights into the roots of their distress, allowing for a fundamental reorganization of their psychological structure and the freeing of previously trapped energy.

- Cognitive Reframing (Cognitive Behavioral Therapy - CBT)

Focusing on the present, cognitive reframing teaches individuals to identify, challenge, and ultimately change distorted or unhelpful thought patterns that contribute to emotional distress. By recognizing "cognitive distortions" (e.g., catastrophizing, black-and-white thinking), individuals learn to adopt more balanced, realistic, and positive perspectives, leading to healthier emotional responses and behavioral choices.

- Narrative Healing

This therapeutic approach emphasizes the power of storytelling. Individuals are encouraged to articulate and re-examine their life narratives, not just as a sequence of events, but as a constructed story through which they understand themselves and their experiences. By identifying dominant stories that may be limiting or disempowering, clients can "re-author" their narratives, integrating past experiences in new ways, finding new meaning, and empowering themselves as the active, resilient protagonists of their own lives.

Often, a blend of these methodologies provides the most comprehensive support, allowing for both deep foundational work and practical, immediate coping strategies.

Nutritional and Holistic Approaches: Nurturing the Mind-Body Connection

True healing acknowledges the profound interplay between our emotional state and physical well-being. Holistic approaches emphasize that the body is not merely a vessel but an intelligent system deeply influenced by our thoughts and feelings.

◈ How Emotions Affect the Body

Chronic stress, unaddressed trauma, and persistent negative emotions can manifest physically through inflammation, digestive issues (e.g., irritable bowel syndrome), hormonal imbalances (e.g., adrenal fatigue), weakened immune function, and exacerbated pain conditions. The enteric nervous system (the "second brain" in the gut) is particularly susceptible to emotional states, linking gut health directly to mood and cognitive function.

◈ Nutritional and Holistic Strategies

This dimension of healing focuses on supporting the body's innate capacity for self-regulation and repair. This includes:

o Nutritionally Dense Diets:

Emphasizing whole, unprocessed foods, ample hydration, and limiting inflammatory agents like sugar and processed fats to optimize gut health, neurotransmitter production, and cellular function.

o Mindfulness and Meditation

Practices that cultivate present moment awareness, reduce stress, regulate the nervous system, and foster a peaceful inner state.

o Movement and Exercise

Regular physical activity, from gentle yoga to vigorous cardio, releases endorphins, reduces stress hormones, improves circulation, and enhances overall vitality.

o Restorative Sleep

Prioritizing consistent, quality sleep as a fundamental pillar for physical and mental restoration.

o Connection with Nature

Spending time outdoors to reduce stress, improve mood, and foster a sense of groundedness.

o Complementary Therapies

Such as acupuncture, herbal medicine, massage therapy, or energy healing, all aimed at restoring balance and supporting the body's natural healing processes.

Nutritional and Holistic Strategies for Addressing Emotional Indigestion: A Therapist's Perspective

As a mental health professional, I recognize that emotional indigestion is a complex and often overlooked aspect of mental and physical well-being. This phenomenon manifests when individuals experience difficulty digesting their emotions, leading to feelings of discomfort, overwhelm, or stagnation. Addressing emotional indigestion requires a comprehensive, holistic approach that not only considers psychological factors but also emphasizes the foundational role of physical health—particularly nutrition and lifestyle habits—in supporting the body's innate capacity for self-regulation and repair.

From a therapeutic standpoint, integrating nutritional and holistic strategies into treatment plans can significantly enhance emotional resilience and foster deeper healing. These strategies are rooted in the understanding that our emotional health is intimately connected to our physical state, especially gut health, neurotransmitter balance, and cellular function. As such, guiding patients towards nutritionally dense diets and mindful lifestyle adjustments can facilitate a more effective and sustainable healing process.

Nutritionally Dense Diets and Their Role in Emotional Healing

A cornerstone of holistic health is the implementation of nutritionally dense diets. These diets prioritize whole, unprocessed foods that are rich in vital nutrients, supporting optimal bodily functions—particularly those related to mood regulation and emotional stability. As a therapist, I advise patients to focus on incorporating a variety of colorful vegetables, fruits, whole grains, lean proteins, nuts, and seeds into their daily intake. These foods provide essential vitamins, minerals, and antioxidants necessary for neurotransmitter synthesis and overall brain health.

Hydration is another critical component. Adequate water intake ensures proper digestion, toxin elimination, and cellular function, all of which influence emotional clarity and stability. I often recommend patients establish consistent hydration routines, such as starting their day with a glass of water and carrying a water bottle throughout the day.

Limiting inflammatory agents is equally important. Excessive sugar, processed fats, and artificial additives can disrupt gut microbiota balance, increase systemic inflammation, and impair neurotransmitter production—factors that can exacerbate emotional distress. Educating patients about reading labels and reducing consumption of processed foods can lead to tangible improvements in mood and emotional resilience.

Gut Health and Its Connection to Emotional Well-being

Emerging research underscores the pivotal role of gut health in emotional regulation—a concept often referred to as the gut-brain axis. An imbalance in gut microbiota can lead to increased inflammation and decreased production of neurotransmitters like serotonin and dopamine, which are vital for mood stability. As a therapist, I emphasize the importance of supporting gut health through diet and lifestyle choices.

Encouraging patients to include probiotic-rich foods such as yogurt, kefir, sauerkraut, and kimchi can help restore microbial balance. Additionally, prebiotic foods like garlic, onions, and asparagus foster the growth of beneficial bacteria. Reducing intake of refined sugars and processed foods minimizes dysbiosis, thereby diminishing emotional turbulence linked to gut inflammation.

Mindfulness and Emotional Self-Regulation

While nutrition forms a foundational aspect of holistic healing, mindfulness practices complement dietary strategies by fostering awareness of emotional and physical states. Mindfulness—through meditation, deep breathing exercises, or body scans—can help individuals identify emotional indigestion as it occurs, allowing for timely intervention and processing. As a therapist, I often incorporate mindfulness training to empower patients to observe their emotional responses without judgment, creating space for self-compassion and clarity.

Furthermore, mindful eating—paying close attention to the sensory experience of each bite—can enhance digestion and promote a more harmonious relationship with food and emotions. This practice encourages slowing down, savoring, and recognizing emotional cues related to hunger and fullness, thereby reducing emotional over- or under-eating.

Holistic Lifestyle Adjustments for Supporting Self-Regulation

Beyond diet and mindfulness, lifestyle factors such as adequate sleep, regular physical activity, and stress management are integral to addressing emotional indigestion. Sleep deprivation impairs emotional processing and increases vulnerability to distress, while physical activity releases endorphins that elevate mood and reduce anxiety. Stress-reduction techniques such as yoga, tai chi, or engaging in hobbies can further support the body's self-healing mechanisms.

Therapeutic Implementation and Patient Support

In clinical practice, my approach involves tailoring these nutritional and holistic strategies to align with each patient's unique circumstances, preferences, and cultural background. I emphasize education, gradual change, and fostering a sense of agency in managing emotional indigestion. Collaboration with nutritionists or integrative health practitioners can enhance the effectiveness of these interventions.

Moreover, I monitor patients' progress through regular check-ins, encouraging reflective journaling about their emotional and physical experiences. This integrated approach helps patients develop a deeper understanding of how their lifestyle choices influence their emotional health, empowering them to implement sustainable changes.

Addressing emotional indigestion requires a multidimensional approach that recognizes the interconnectedness of mind and body. By focusing on nutritionally dense diets, gut health, mindfulness, and holistic lifestyle adjustments, therapists can significantly support their patients in restoring emotional balance and resilience. These strategies empower individuals to tap into their innate capacity for self-regulation and repair, ultimately fostering a more harmonious and healthy relationship with their emotions and overall well-being.

Practical Steps: Cultivating Self-Empowerment

Beyond therapeutic and holistic interventions, healing requires actionable steps that empower individuals to take an active role in their well-being:

◈ Self-Recognition

This foundational step involves developing acute awareness of one's inner world – understanding emotional triggers, identifying recurring thought patterns, recognizing self-sabotaging behaviors, and acknowledging personal needs. It's about cultivating self-compassion and curiosity rather than judgment, allowing for honest introspection that paves the way for change.

◈ Boundary Setting

A crucial act of self-preservation, boundary setting involves defining and communicating one's emotional, physical, and energetic limits. This includes learning to say "no," protecting personal time and space, and disengaging from relationships or situations that are draining or disrespectful. Effective boundaries foster healthier relationships and conserve vital energy for self-care and growth.

◈ Reclaiming Joy

Healing is not merely the absence of pain but the proactive pursuit of moments of light, purpose, and genuine happiness. This involves rediscovering passions, engaging in activities that bring a sense of flow and satisfaction, cultivating gratitude for simple pleasures, fostering meaningful connections, and allowing for playfulness and spontaneity – re-establishing a future-oriented hope and agency in one's life.

Case Examples of Healing and Transformation

While names and specific details are altered for privacy, these composite examples illustrate the profound impact of embracing healing pathways:

◈ Elara's Journey:

Elara, a 35-year-old marketing executive, suffered from chronic anxiety and debilitating panic attacks, rooted in unaddressed childhood trauma. Through a combination of psychoanalysis, which helped her understand and process early experiences, and cognitive reframing, which allowed her to challenge her catastrophic thinking, Elara began to untangle the knots of her past. Simultaneously, she learned to practice mindfulness and set firm boundaries with demanding colleagues, protecting her energetic well-being. Over two years, Elara transformed from a high-strung individual constantly on edge to someone embodying inner peace, capable of navigating stress with resilience, and cultivating deeply meaningful relationships.

◈ Marcus's Transformation

Marcus, a 50-year-old artist, experienced persistent fatigue, digestive issues, and a general sense of malaise, which doctors attributed to stress. While traditional medicine offered limited solutions, Marcus embarked on a holistic healing pathway. He adopted an anti-inflammatory diet, significantly reduced processed foods and sugar, and incorporated daily meditation and gentle yoga. Narrative healing helped him reframe his artistic "struggles" as a creative process rather than personal failure, alleviating immense self-imposed pressure. Within 18 months, Marcus reported a dramatic increase in energy, resolution of his digestive complaints, and a renewed passion for his art, demonstrating the powerful impact of addressing the body and spirit in conjunction with the mind.

These Healing Pathways, whether pursued individually or in combination, offer a beacon of hope and a practical roadmap for anyone seeking not just to alleviate suffering, but to flourish and live a life of wholeness, purpose, and joy.

Reflection Questions

1. What healing method speaks to me most—talking therapy, journaling, prayer, community?

1. What small act of independence can I practice this week?

Exercise

- Journaling Prompt: Write one page about a time you overcame fear in your life.
- What strength did you discover then that you can use now?
- Small Independence Step: Do one daily task (cooking, walking, making a decision) purely for yourself. Write how it feels.

Chapter 10: Reclaiming the Self

Key Arguments

- Rediscovering identity beyond attachment.
- Self-sourced happiness: moving from dependency to autonomy.
- Building resilience: living whole before, during, and after relationships.
- Hope for a new narrative of love and selfhood.
- The goal is not only to leave unhealthy relationships but to rediscover one's full identity.
- Happiness sourced internally is more sustainable than dependency.
- Relationships can then be entered freely, without indigestion.
- This is not only personal healing but collective healing for communities.

Examples

- A woman who left a marriage and later became a community mentor for young girls.
- A therapist who, after resolving her own indigestion, became more effective at helping others.

Reclaiming the Self: A Journey Towards Wholeness

Reclaiming the Self is not merely a phase, but a profound and transformative journey towards authentic living, particularly after experiences where one's identity may have merged or been overshadowed by external relationships or expectations. It signifies a courageous pivot back to one's core essence, fostering an unshakeable inner foundation regardless of life's fluctuating circumstances.

Central to this transformative process is rediscovering identity beyond attachment. This involves consciously peeling back the layers of who we thought we "should" be, or who we became in response to others, to unearth the unique individual beneath. It means identifying one's core values, passions, aspirations, and unique perspectives that exist independently of any romantic partner, family role, or social group. It's about recognizing that one's worth and validity are not derived from external validation or a coupled status, but from an inherent, autonomous sense of self.

This pursuit naturally leads to cultivating self-sourced happiness, moving decisively from dependency to autonomy. Instead of relying on another person or external circumstances to provide joy, fulfillment, or emotional stability, this phase focuses on tapping into an internal wellspring of contentment. It's about developing the personal agency to create one's own joy, deriving satisfaction from personal achievements, self-care, intrinsic interests, and a deep appreciation for one's own company. This shift from an "if-then" happiness model (e.g., "I'll be happy if I have X person") to an "I am" happiness empowers individuals with emotional independence, ensuring that their well-being is not contingent on another's presence or actions.

Crucially, this foundational strength extends to building resilience: living whole before, during, and after relationships. This means cultivating an intrinsic sense of completeness and integrity that precedes entering any significant emotional bond. Before a relationship, one is a sturdy, self-sufficient entity.

During a relationship, this wholeness allows for healthy interdependence – two complete individuals choosing to share their lives, rather than two halves attempting to create a whole. It fosters the ability to maintain one's distinct identity, boundaries, and individual pursuits even while deeply connected to another. And critically, after a relationship ends, this robust inner fortress enables one to navigate the inevitable pain and transition without shattering, to heal comprehensively, and to emerge with an intact, resilient sense of self, capable of thriving independently once more.

Ultimately, this entire process culminates in a profound hope for a new narrative of love and selfhood. It's a vision that rejects outdated scripts of codependency, self-sacrifice, or the notion that love completes an incomplete person. Instead, it champions a empowered paradigm where authentic love arises from two whole, self-actualized individuals who choose to unite, fostering mutual growth, respect, and shared joy, rather than seeking to fill a void in one another. This new narrative celebrates self-love as the prerequisite for healthy romantic love, promising a future where relationships are enriching additions to an already fulfilling life, rather than the singular definition or sole source of one's identity and happiness.

Conclusion: Towards Emotional Freedom

- Summarize the journey from dependency to selfhood.
- Call to readers: confront your indigestions, choose healing.
- Vision: communities where people live whole, healthy, and free of silent suffering.

- Stories/Case Vignettes: Short narratives from women, men, or even therapists to illustrate emotional indigestion.
- Reflection Questions: At the end of each chapter for reader engagement.
- Practical Exercises: Journaling prompts, self-assessment checklists, small steps toward emotional independence.

This journey, which began amidst the often-unseen burdens of emotional dependency, now culminates in the vibrant prospect of authentic selfhood.

We have navigated the intricate landscape of 'emotional indigestions,' dissecting how unexpressed feelings, unresolved traumas, and unacknowledged wounds manifest as silent suffering, anxiety, and even tangible physical discomfort. Through the shared vulnerability of diverse stories and case vignettes—be they from women, men, or even the insightful perspectives of therapists—we've illuminated the universal nature of these struggles, revealing that you are not alone in your experience.

Now, as you reach the close of these pages, the true work begins. I extend a heartfelt call to you, the reader: confront your own emotional indigestions with courage and compassion. This is not merely about passive understanding; it's about making a conscious, deliberate choice towards profound healing.

The tools are within your grasp: reflect deeply on the questions posed at the end of each chapter, engage earnestly with the practical exercises, utilize the journaling prompts for self-discovery, and leverage the self-assessment checklists to chart your progress. Take those small, deliberate steps toward true emotional independence, knowing that each one builds upon the last.

My deepest hope is for a future where the pervasive weight of silent suffering is lifted from our collective shoulders. Imagine communities transformed into vibrant ecosystems where individuals live whole, healthy, and emotionally articulate lives, unburdened by the unprocessed past.

Let us collectively strive towards this vision, fostering a world where every person feels truly free to embrace their authentic self, navigate their inner world with grace, and contribute their full, unencumbered spirit to the tapestry of human experience. The path to emotional freedom is a continuous unfolding, and it begins with your brave, beautiful choice.

Reclaiming the Self: A Journey Towards Wholeness – case study

The streets of London buzzed with a relentless energy, a stark contrast to the quiet introspection Lesiba Jacob often sought in the depths of his mind. Born and raised in Mokopane, a small but vibrant town nestled within the Mogalakwena Municipality, Lesiba had always carried an undercurrent of longing—not just to escape the confines of his roots but to find an authentic version of himself buried beneath layers of expectation, duty, and external validation.

Lesiba's story was one of unraveling, a long winding path toward reclaiming the self. His journey was not a straight line but a tumultuous voyage through cultural bonds, personal loss, and societal pressures. It was a quest to forge an unshakeable inner foundation, especially after experiences where his identity had merged or been overshadowed by external relationships or expectations.

Lesiba's early years in Mokopane were filled with the warmth of tradition. His grandmother, Madam Brooks, was a pillar in their community, known for her wisdom and healing prowess. She often told him stories of their ancestors, emphasizing the importance of knowing oneself beyond societal roles.

"Lesiba," she would say, "the world will try to tell you who you are, but only you can truly know your essence. Never lose that."

Yet, as Lesiba grew older and moved to London for university, the outside world's expectations began to weigh heavily on him. He threw himself into his studies—psychology, as he believed understanding the mind might help him unravel his own tangled feelings. But amidst the busy cityscape, he felt increasingly disconnected from who he was.

His return trips to Mokopane became infrequent, and when he did visit, he often found himself overwhelmed by the lingering shadows of cultural expectations and familial duties. His grandmother's voice echoed in his mind, urging him to reconnect with his roots and his true self.

The next significant chapter unfolded when Lesiba moved to New York for a postgraduate program. The bustling metropolis widened his horizons but also intensified his internal conflicts. He started seeing a therapist there, Dr. Evelyn Carter, who specialized in identity and trauma.

"Lesiba, tell me about your sense of self," Dr. Carter prompted in one session.

"I think I lost it somewhere along the way," he admitted. "I feel like I'm living for others, not for myself. I've always been told who to be, how to act. I don't even recognize myself anymore."

Through therapy, Lesiba began to piece together the fragments of his identity. The journey was arduous—filled with moments of doubt and vulnerability, but also awakening.

One day, in a quiet moment during a visit to London, Lesiba received an unexpected call from Lucia, an old friend and fellow traveler of life's complexities. She was now living in the city and had experienced her own journey of rediscovery.

"Lesiba, I've been thinking," Lucia said softly. "Sometimes, we have to strip away everything—our roles, our titles, even our beliefs—to find what's left. That's where the real self resides."

Lesiba listened intently, feeling a flicker of hope ignite within him.

The turning point arrived during a visit back to Mokopane, where Lesiba sat at his grandmother's side in her humble home. They discussed his struggles, the layers he wanted to shed, and the core he longed to grasp.

"Grandmother," he asked, "how do I know when I've truly found myself?"

"You will feel it," she replied gently. "When you are no longer living in the shadows of others' expectations but standing in your own light. When your actions align with your truth, and your heart feels at peace. That's when you reclaim yourself."

Inspired by her words, Lesiba embarked on a deliberate journey of self-reclamation. He sought out traditional healers, including Madam Brooks herself, who guided him through rituals of cleansing and renewal. He visited the Mogalakwena Clinic, where he volunteered and reconnected with his cultural roots, and later traveled to Polokwane Hospital and the Polokwane Health Department, where he volunteered in mental health outreach programs.

Throughout this process, Lesiba learned to distinguish his authentic voice from the cacophony of external influences. He began to embrace vulnerability, acknowledging his fears and insecurities as part of his human experience.

Meanwhile, in London, Lesiba's life took a new turn when he met Melita, a perceptive artist whose work explored themes of identity and self-discovery. Their conversations often delved into the essence of being true to oneself, beyond societal masks.

"You see," Melita said during one of their discussions, "reclaiming the self is like painting over a faded mural. It takes patience, courage, and sometimes, erasing what was there before to make space for something real."

Lesiba nodded, finally understanding that his journey toward wholeness was not about perfection but about embracing all parts of himself—the pain, the joy, the contradictions.

Over time, Lesiba's life in London blossomed with newfound authenticity. He started speaking at community centers about his experiences, sharing his story of reclaiming the self. His relationships grew richer because they were rooted in honesty and vulnerability.

One evening, as he sat alone in a café, reflecting on his journey, his phone rang. It was his mother from Mokopane.

"Lesiba, my son," she said warmly, "we are proud of you. You have come back to yourself, and that is the greatest gift. Remember, your true strength lies in your authenticity."

Tears welled in Lesiba's eyes as he responded, "Thank you, Mama. I am finally beginning to understand that *reclaiming the self is the most beautiful journey of all."*

His story was far from over, but he knew now that regaining his identity beyond attachment was a lifelong pursuit, one that required courage, patience, and unwavering love for himself.

As he looked out over the London skyline, Lesiba felt a profound peace. He had begun to reclaim his story, and with it, the wholeness he had always sought.

The journey towards authentic living was, after all, the most remarkable adventure of all.

The Journey from Dependency to Selfhood

As a therapist, I have witnessed countless individuals trapped in the silent suffering of emotional indigestion. This condition, often overlooked, manifests as internal turmoil—unprocessed feelings, unresolved conflicts, and unmet needs—that impair one's capacity to live authentically and independently. The journey from dependency towards selfhood is a transformative process that requires courage, awareness, and intentional healing.

Emotional indigestion begins subtly. Perhaps it starts with a recurring sense of dissatisfaction, anxiety, or overwhelm that seems disproportionate to current circumstances. Left unacknowledged, these feelings fester, leading to behaviors rooted in avoidance, dependency, or emotional numbness. From a therapeutic standpoint, recognizing the early signs of emotional indigestion is crucial. It signals a need for deeper exploration and active engagement with one's inner world.

This chapter aims to guide both clinicians and individuals on the path towards emotional freedom—confronting the indigestions that hinder authentic living, choosing healing over avoidance, and envisioning communities where people live whole, healthy, and free from silent suffering.

The Spectrum of Emotional Indigestion: Recognizing the Signs

In my clinical practice, I observe that emotional indigestion often presents as:

- Chronic Anxiety or Restlessness

A persistent feeling of unease without a clear external cause.

- Emotional Numbing

Detachment from feelings or a tendency to suppress emotional experiences.

- Dependency Patterns

Relying excessively on others for validation or decision-making.

- Recurrent Conflicts

Repeating the same relationship or personal issues without resolution.

- Physical Manifestations

Stress-related ailments such as tension headaches, gastrointestinal discomfort, or fatigue, often linked to unresolved emotional states.

Understanding these signs is the first step towards addressing emotional indigestion. It requires cultivating mindfulness and self-awareness—skills I teach patients to develop during therapy.

The Spectrum of Emotional Indigestion: Recognizing the Signs

As a mental health professional, I often encounter clients presenting with subtle yet pervasive signs of emotional indigestion — a term I use to describe the internal discomfort and dysregulation caused by unprocessed or poorly managed emotional experiences. Recognizing the spectrum of emotional indigestion is crucial for effective intervention, as these symptoms can significantly impair an individual's psychological well-being and overall functioning.

In my clinical practice, emotional indigestion frequently manifests in several observable ways. Among the most common are chronic anxiety or restlessness. Clients may describe an ongoing sense of unease, agitation, or nervous energy that persists despite the absence of identifiable external stressors. This persistent internal tension often feels like an internal storm, yet it remains elusive in terms of specific causes. Such anxiety can be debilitating, leading to difficulty concentrating, sleep disturbances, and avoidance behaviors.

Another prominent presentation is emotional numbing—an avoidance strategy that involves detachment from feelings or a conscious suppression of emotional experiences. Clients may report feeling disconnected from their emotions, experiencing a sense of flatness, or struggling to access joy or sadness. This numbing serves as a protective mechanism but ultimately hampers emotional processing and hampers authentic engagement with oneself and others.

Dependency patterns also frequently indicate emotional indigestion. Clients may rely excessively on external validation, seeking reassurance or approval from others to feel worthy or secure. This dependency often stems from underlying issues of self-esteem or unresolved emotional wounds. It can reinforce feelings of vulnerability and hinder the development of internal resilience.

From a therapeutic perspective, addressing emotional indigestion requires a nuanced and compassionate approach. The first step involves careful recognition and validation of these signs. Encouraging clients to articulate their internal experiences without judgment can foster greater self-awareness. Active listening and empathetic inquiry help to uncover underlying emotional conflicts or unmet needs that contribute to their distress.

Once these signs are identified, a tailored intervention plan can be implemented. Cognitive-behavioral strategies are often effective in helping clients develop awareness of maladaptive thought patterns linked to anxiety or dependency. Mindfulness-based techniques can support clients in becoming more attuned to their emotional states, promoting acceptance rather than avoidance. For clients experiencing emotional numbing, interventions such as emotion-focused therapy or experiential exercises can facilitate access to suppressed feelings, encouraging emotional processing and integration.

Building emotional resilience is fundamental. This involves helping clients develop internal resources—such as self-compassion, assertiveness, and emotional regulation skills—that reduce reliance on external validation and improve their ability to tolerate discomfort. Psychoeducation about the nature of emotions and their function can demystify feelings and reduce stigma or fear associated with experiencing vulnerability.

Moreover, addressing underlying attachment issues or unresolved trauma is often essential. Techniques such as trauma-informed care or working through attachment wounds can help clients establish a more secure internal attachment system, decreasing dependence on external validation and fostering emotional independence.

Throughout therapy, it is vital to create a safe and supportive environment where clients feel comfortable exploring difficult emotions without fear of judgment. Patience and consistency are key, as emotional indigestion often develops over years and cannot be resolved overnight. Small, incremental steps—such as journaling feelings, practicing mindfulness, or engaging in emotion-focused interventions—can lead to meaningful change over time.

In summary, emotional indigestion manifests through various interconnected signs, including chronic anxiety, emotional numbing, and dependency patterns. As clinicians, our role is to recognize these manifestations, validate clients' experiences, and employ a comprehensive, empathetic approach to facilitate emotional awareness, regulation, and resilience. With sustained effort and tailored interventions, clients can achieve a more balanced emotional life—transforming internal discomfort into growth and self-understanding.

Confronting Your Indigestions: A Call to Action

I urge readers to confront their emotional indigestions directly. Avoidance perpetuates suffering, while acknowledgment opens the door to healing. Ask yourself:

- Are there feelings I refuse to face? Why?
- Do I rely excessively on others to feel validated or secure?
- How do my emotional patterns affect my relationships and well-being?
- What parts of myself am I neglecting or suppressing?

In therapy, I often guide clients through these reflections, creating a safe space where they can explore their inner landscape without judgment. Recognizing emotional indigestion is not a sign of weakness but a step towards reclaiming personal sovereignty.

As a therapist, I often encounter clients who grapple with what I refer to as "emotional indigestion"—an internal state characterized by unresolved feelings, suppressed emotions, and unprocessed emotional discomfort. Much like physical indigestion signals a disturbance in our digestive system, emotional indigestion reflects a disruption within our psychological and emotional well-being. Left unaddressed, it can lead to chronic stress, relational difficulties, and a diminished sense of inner peace. My professional stance emphasizes that confronting these underlying emotional issues directly is essential for genuine healing and growth.

Avoidance, whether conscious or unconscious, perpetuates suffering. When we refuse to face uncomfortable feelings, they do not simply disappear; instead, they often manifest in maladaptive ways—such as irritability, anxiety, or withdrawal—which can further entrench emotional distress. Conversely, acknowledgment of our feelings creates the fertile ground necessary for healing. Recognizing and accepting our emotional experiences is a courageous act that opens the door to understanding ourselves more deeply and fostering resilience.

In therapy, I guide clients through a process of honest self-inquiry. I encourage them to ask themselves pivotal questions:

- Are there feelings I refuse to face? Why?
- Do I rely excessively on others to feel validated or secure?
- How do my emotional patterns affect my relationships and well-being?
- What parts of myself am I neglecting or suppressing?

These questions serve as catalysts for introspection, helping clients identify patterns of avoidance, dependency, or self-neglect that may be fueling their emotional indigestion.

When working with clients on this issue, I emphasize a compassionate and non-judgmental approach. Confronting difficult emotions can be uncomfortable, but it is a necessary step toward genuine healing. I encourage clients to create a safe internal space where they can explore their feelings without fear of judgment or shame. Techniques such as mindfulness, emotion-focused therapy, and gentle inquiry can facilitate this process. For example, mindfulness helps clients observe their emotional states with curiosity rather than avoidance, fostering acceptance and reducing resistance.

Furthermore, I stress the importance of developing emotional literacy—learning to identify, label, and express feelings accurately. Many individuals avoid certain emotions because they lack familiarity or fear their intensity. Building emotional vocabulary and practicing expressive techniques, such as journaling or dialogue, can empower clients to process emotions rather than suppress them.

An essential component of addressing emotional indigestion involves examining underlying beliefs and narratives. Clients often hold subconscious assumptions—such as "I shouldn't feel this way" or "Expressing emotions is a sign of weakness"—which reinforce avoidance and suppression. Challenging and reframing these beliefs allow clients to see their emotions as valid and integral to their human experience.

In addition, I work with clients to recognize how their emotional patterns influence their interpersonal relationships. For example, chronic avoidance might lead to emotional distance, while dependency on others for validation can result in codependency or feelings of emptiness. Awareness of these patterns offers opportunities for change—fostering healthier communication, boundary-setting, and self-validation.

Ultimately, healing from emotional indigestion requires a willingness to explore the often uncomfortable truths within ourselves. It involves patience, compassion, and ongoing commitment to self-awareness. As a therapist, I serve as a guide and support system on this journey, helping clients develop the skills necessary to confront their emotional indigestions directly and transform them into sources of growth and resilience.

In conclusion, I urge each reader to reflect deeply on their own emotional landscape. Avoidance sustains suffering; acknowledgment paves the way for healing. Embrace your feelings with kindness and curiosity. Recognize the patterns that hinder your well-being, and take proactive steps toward understanding and integrating every part of yourself. Only through honest confrontation can true emotional health be achieved.

Strategies for Healing: From Dependency to Selfhood

When working with patients, I employ a multifaceted approach:

1. Building Emotional Awareness: Cultivating mindfulness practices to identify and name feelings as they arise.

In the realm of psychoanalytic therapy, emotional awareness is the cornerstone of healing. Mindfulness practices, such as meditation and body scanning, help clients slow down and connect with their emotional states. A case study of Sarah, a 32-year-old teacher, illustrates this. Experiencing chronic anxiety, Sarah struggled to articulate her feelings. Through guided mindfulness exercises, she learned to identify sensations tied to specific emotions—tightness in her chest signaling anxiety, or warmth in her heart indicating joy. Over time, as she became adept at naming her feelings, Sarah reported increased emotional regulation and a deeper understanding of her internal experiences. This newfound awareness allowed her to express her emotions constructively, transforming her relationships and enhancing her overall well-being.

Processing Unfinished Business: Encouraging clients to explore past experiences that contribute to current emotional patterns.

Unfinished business often manifests as unresolved issues from the past that hinder emotional growth. In psychoanalytic therapy, addressing these lingering concerns can be transformative. Consider the case of Mark, a 45-year-old man grappling with recurrent fears of abandonment. Through exploration, it emerged that Mark's childhood experiences with an emotionally distant father shaped his current relationships. Using psychodynamic techniques, Mark revisited these formative experiences, allowing him to articulate his feelings of hurt and betrayal. This process of exploration not only facilitated emotional release but also fostered a sense of closure. As Mark confronted his past, he began to recognize patterns in his adult relationships and worked towards healthier connections. By processing unfinished business, clients like Mark can break free from the constraints of their past, paving the way for emotional healing and growth.

Developing Self-Compassion

Teaching self-kindness to counteract shame or self-criticism linked to emotional indigestion.

1. Establishing Boundaries

Assisting individuals in setting healthy limits that promote self-respect and independence.

1. Fostering Authentic Expression

Supporting clients in communicating their needs and feelings honestly.

1. Encouraging Inner Child Work

Addressing unmet needs from childhood that may underlie current dependency patterns.

1. Creating Supportive Environments

Facilitating group or community connections where emotional honesty is valued and vulnerability is safe.

#	Name / Location	Freud's Construct	Jungian Archetype	Cultural / Healing Intervention	Key Emot Indig Mani
1	Jacob, New York, USA	Displacement, Transference	Shadow (repressed vulnerability)	Psychoanalytic therapy, dream analysis, support groups	Anxi overv diges issues
2	Emeka, Lagos, Nigeria	Repression of vulnerability	Invincible Provider (collective archetype)	Counseling with rituals, family therapy	Hype inson relati tensic
3	Dimitris, Athens, Greece	Repression of authentic desire	Anima (suppressed creativity/ emotion)	Therapy, creative workshops	Gastr fatigu chror dissat
4	Thomas, London, UK	Projection, Transference	Shadow (unacknowledged emotional need)	Psychoanalytic therapy, mindfulness, journaling	Emo withc relati tensic
5	Luke, Sydney, Australia	Repression of dependency	Anima (ignored emotional side)	Therapy, men's support circles	Chro fatigu relate
6	Nomsa, Harare, Zimbabwe	Repression of anger/grief	Endurance/Silence (intergenerational)	Church-based support circles, rituals	Hype chror anxie
7	Amina, Accra, Ghana	Compulsive caregiving (repetition compulsion)	Nurturing Mother (collective archetype)	Psychoeducation, empowerment, ritual catharsis	Anxi relati deper supp: ange

8	Fatima, Gabon	Repression of autonomy	Endurance/Silence (intergenerational)	Traditional healing, communal storytelling	Hype stress- illnes
9	Elias, Johannesburg, South Africa	Unresolved dependency	Shadow (repressed empathy)	Therapy, men's groups	Anxie emoti withd
10	Sofia, Rural Italy	Repression of desire	Dutiful Spouse (archetype)	Individual therapy, expressive arts, peer groups	Chro dissat stress
11	Pastor Jean, Gabon	Transference, Repression	Shadow (fear of inadequacy/ loneliness)	Psychoanalytic supervision, ritual, prayer	Relati fear, b emoti repres
12	Therapist Helen, London, UK	Transference, Repression	Shadow (unintegrated fears)	Supervision, therapy, shadow work	Emot exhau relatio depen

Key Notes for the Table:

This process often involves confronting uncomfortable truths, but it ultimately leads to a stronger sense of self—an essential foundation for emotional freedom.

Stories and Case Essays: Illustrations of Emotional Indigestion

Vignette 1: Maria's Journey from Numbness to Authenticity

Maria, a 35-year-old woman, came to therapy feeling disconnected from her feelings. She described herself as "emotionally numb," often suppressing anger and sadness. Through exploration, Maria uncovered a childhood of emotional invalidation, where expressing vulnerability was discouraged. As she learned to acknowledge and articulate her feelings, she gradually moved away from dependency on others' approval and embraced her authentic self. Today, Maria lives with greater self-awareness and emotional clarity.

Vignette 2: James's Dependency Pattern

James, a 42-year-old man, relied heavily on his partner for decision-making, fearing rejection or abandonment. His emotional indigestion manifested as anxiety and codependency. In therapy, James worked on building self-trust and understanding the roots of his insecurities. With support, he developed internal resources and boundaries that fostered independence. His relationships became more balanced, and he experienced a newfound sense of agency.

Vignette 3: Therapist's Reflection

As a therapist, I recall a client who initially avoided emotional discomfort at all costs. Through gentle confrontation and creating a safe space, I guided him to confront his fears of vulnerability. Witnessing his transformation from emotional suppression to openness reaffirmed my belief in the power of confronting indigestion directly. Healing is possible when we face our inner truths with compassion.

The Psychoanalytic Journey Through Emotional Indigestion

Emotional indigestion, much like its physical counterpart, is the psyche's signal that something has not been fully metabolized. In Freud's view, psychic conflict arises when instinctual drives, unacknowledged desires, or unresolved traumas remain lodged in the unconscious, unintegrated into conscious awareness. They return as symptoms: restlessness, heaviness, anxiety, or the sense of being "stuck." Healing therefore requires a turning inward, a willingness to encounter the repressed material and to grant it language, form, and meaning.

Rediscovering the Self

When we ask, "What part of myself have I rediscovered in this journey?" we are invoking Freud's central insight—that the self is not a static entity but a layered structure of id, ego, and superego, often in tension. In the process of therapy, fragments of the self that had been cast off into the unconscious return to consciousness. Perhaps it is the playful child who once delighted in drawing but was silenced by a stern parental voice. Perhaps it is the passionate lover who dared to desire, but later repressed that desire in the name of duty. Or perhaps it is the confident dreamer whose ambitions were dismissed as impossible, and so became buried under self-doubt.

To rediscover these lost parts is not to fabricate a "new" identity, but to reclaim what was always ours, waiting beneath the defenses we built for survival. Freud called this the work of remembering and repeating—remembering what was lost, repeating what was suppressed, but now in a new and conscious form. Healing begins when we can look at these disowned fragments not as foreign intrusions but as integral aspects of our wholeness.

Commitment to the Self

The second question—"What one commitment will I make to myself today?"—invites the ego to act as mediator. In Freud's structural model, the ego negotiates between the instinctual demands of the id, the moral injunctions of the superego, and the realities of the external world. A commitment, then, is an ego-function: a conscious decision to integrate rather than split off the conflicting parts of the psyche.

If the superego whispers, "You must always sacrifice for others," while the id cries, "I want to live and enjoy freely," the ego's task is not to eliminate either voice, but to hold them in dialogue. The commitment might be as simple as: I will give myself 20 minutes of uninterrupted solitude today, or I will speak one truth, even if my voice trembles. These are not grand resolutions but subtle ego-strengthening acts. Over time, these acts accumulate, building a self that is not governed solely by repression or guilt but by conscious choice.

The Small Step: Promise to the Future Self

Freud emphasized the working-through process—the gradual revisiting of conflicts in order to loosen their grip. Writing a promise to one's future self, and sealing it, is an act of working-through. Symbolically, it places the unconscious desire into material form. The sealed promise becomes a transitional object, holding the tension between present struggle and future transformation.

For example, one might write: "When doubt rises, I will remember that my worth is not dependent on perfection. I promise to return to the part of myself that seeks joy, even in small things." The very act of sealing the promise mirrors the psychoanalytic act of containing and binding psychic energy, preventing it from dispersing chaotically. When reopened later, the promise serves as a mirror of continuity, proof that despite fragmentation, the self remains tethered across time.

Affirmation: Freedom, Healing, Wholeness

Finally, the affirmation—"I choose freedom, healing, and wholeness"—is more than a positive statement. From a Freudian lens, it is a counter-suggestion, a way of rewriting the internalized narratives of the superego that often echo parental prohibitions or societal constraints. To say I choose is to assert the ego's agency in the face of unconscious repetition compulsion—the tendency to reenact old wounds.

Freedom signifies liberation from the repetitive grip of repression. Healing suggests the integration of split-off material, the capacity to hold both pain and pleasure without denial. Wholeness is the ego's recognition that the self includes contradictions, wounds, and desires, yet remains a coherent totality. This affirmation is not a denial of suffering but a reclamation of agency within it.

⟐ Reflection

- What part of myself have I rediscovered in this journey?

- What one commitment will I make to myself today?

◈ Small Step

- Write a short promise to your future self and seal it for reflection later.

⟐ Affirmation

- "I choose freedom, healing, and wholeness."
  ☐ "I said it aloud today"

◈ Notes

(Open blank lined section with heading "Insights I discovered while working through this exercise")

Reader's Reflection

At this stage, I invite you, the reader, to notice: when you rediscover a forgotten part of yourself, what emotions rise—joy, grief, anger, relief? These are signals of psychic energy shifting, the unconscious stirring as it yields its treasures. Write them down without censorship. Freud would remind us that slips, associations, and even what feels "irrelevant" often carry the deepest meaning.

Then, make your commitment not as a burden but as an act of self-love, a gesture of integration. Seal your promise to your future self as though you are both patient and analyst—bearing witness, offering continuity. And as you whisper or write the affirmation, let it resonate as an act of defiance against the tyranny of old prohibitions.

Healing from emotional indigestion is not a one-time purge. It is a slow digestion of psychic life, bite by bite, memory by memory, promise by promise. But in this work, every rediscovered fragment becomes nourishment, every commitment a step toward integration, and every affirmation a declaration of your right to live fully, freely, and whole.

Reflection Questions: Deepening Your Understanding

At the end of each chapter, I invite you to reflect on the following questions:

- What emotional patterns do I notice recurring in my life?
- In what ways might I be avoiding or suppressing difficult feelings?
- How have my dependency behaviors affected my personal growth and relationships?
- What steps can I take today to acknowledge and validate my emotional experiences?
- How can my community support a culture of emotional honesty and healing?

Engaging with these questions fosters self-awareness and empowers you to make conscious choices towards emotional freedom.

Deepening Your Understanding: A Call to Introspective Engagement

As we conclude each chapter of this transformative journey, it's crucial to pause and allow the insights to truly integrate. This is not merely an invitation for passive reflection, but a deliberate call to engage with the material on a deeply personal level. By doing so, you move beyond theoretical knowledge and begin to forge a tangible path towards profound self-awareness and sustainable emotional well-being.

To facilitate this vital process, I invite you to dedicate time and space to thoughtfully consider the following probing questions. These are designed to serve as mirrors, illuminating your inner landscape, and as catalysts, prompting actionable steps toward greater emotional freedom and authentic living:

What emotional patterns do I notice recurring in my life?

This question encourages you to become a keen observer of your internal world. Beyond isolated incidents, consider the larger cycles: Do you consistently react to stress with anger, retreat, or excessive control? Do certain triggers reliably lead to feelings of anxiety, sadness, or joy? Identifying these recurring patterns – whether in your reactions to conflict, in your relationships, or in moments of personal challenge – is the first critical step toward understanding their origins and ultimately, reshaping your habitual responses.

Understanding and Addressing Emotional Indigestion: A Therapist's Perspective on Recognizing Recurring Emotional Patterns

As mental health professionals, one of our primary objectives is to guide clients toward greater self-awareness, particularly regarding their emotional landscapes. A prevalent challenge many individuals face is what can be termed emotional indigestion—a persistent inability to process, digest, and integrate their emotional experiences effectively. This phenomenon often manifests as recurring feelings of discomfort, overwhelm, or distress that seem to cycle through an individual's life, much like indigestion in the physical realm, where unresolved issues linger and disrupt overall well-being.

The Importance of Recognizing Recurring Emotional Patterns

In my clinical practice, I emphasize the significance of cultivating a keen observational stance toward one's internal world. Asking patients, "What emotional patterns do I notice recurring in my life?" serves as a foundational question that promotes introspective awareness. This question encourages clients to move beyond isolated incidents and to consider larger, more systemic cycles—patterns that repeat across different contexts, situations, or relationships.

For example, a client might observe that they tend to react with anger whenever they feel overlooked or undervalued, or that they retreat into silence when faced with confrontation. Others may notice a tendency toward excessive control when they experience feelings of insecurity, or a recurring sense of anxiety triggered by specific situations such as social gatherings or work-related stress. Recognizing these patterns is crucial because they often serve as the underlying emotional currents that influence behavior, perception, and overall mental health.

Understanding Underlying Cycles and Triggers

A key component of addressing emotional indigestion is helping clients identify the larger cycles at play. These are not merely isolated reactions but often part of entrenched emotional schemas or coping mechanisms developed over time. For example, a person might consistently react to stress with anger because this was reinforced in childhood as a way to assert boundaries or gain control.

Furthermore, understanding specific triggers can illuminate how certain external events reliably evoke particular emotional responses—be it anxiety, sadness, or joy. For instance, a client might notice that criticism from others frequently leads to feelings of worthlessness or shame, while achieving a goal might reliably produce feelings of pride and happiness. By mapping these triggers and responses, clients can start to see the patterns that govern their emotional experiences.

Therapeutic Strategies for Managing Emotional Indigestion

From a therapeutic standpoint, addressing emotional indigestion involves a multi-layered approach: 1. Awareness and Mindfulness

The first step in addressing emotional indigestion is cultivating awareness. Many clients arrive in therapy disconnected from their inner world—reacting automatically to stressors rather than consciously experiencing them. As a therapist, I emphasize mindfulness practices that ground clients in the present moment. Body scans, slow intentional breathing, and mindful journaling become tools for tuning into subtle emotional cues. Clients begin to notice the tightening of the chest, the shallow breath, or the restless mind as signals rather than intrusions. Over time, this shift from automatic reaction to mindful observation allows clients to meet their emotions with curiosity rather than fear.

2. Pattern Recognition and Reflection

Once awareness is established, the next step is helping clients identify and trace patterns. Through reflective exercises, narrative therapy, or guided dialogue, I invite clients to map the recurring scenarios that activate emotional pain. "When does the anger return? When do you feel the pull of shame or silence?" These questions uncover not only the triggers but also the embedded stories—family expectations, cultural scripts, or unresolved childhood wounds—that give meaning to their responses. Recognizing these links transforms emotions from random, overwhelming waves into understandable signals rooted in lived experience.

3. Cognitive and Emotional Reprocessing

With patterns visible, the therapeutic work moves into reprocessing. Cognitive-behavioral approaches help reframe deeply held but unhelpful beliefs such as "I am unworthy" or "I must never disappoint." In parallel, emotion-focused techniques create space to safely re-experience and express emotions that may have been long suppressed—grief, anger, longing. Clients learn that emotions, once feared as destructive, are often carrying vital truths about needs, values, and boundaries. This reframing builds resilience and provides healthier strategies for coping.

4. Developing Emotional Literacy

A recurring challenge in therapy is that many clients lack the vocabulary to name what they feel. They may reduce their experience to "good" or "bad," leaving the complexity of their inner life unacknowledged. I guide clients in expanding their emotional vocabulary—distinguishing between irritation and rage, sadness and grief, anxiety and anticipation. The more precisely one can name a feeling, the easier it becomes to validate, process, and communicate it. Emotional literacy is not just academic; it is liberating, as it transforms vague discomfort into language that can be shared and understood.

5. Building Tolerance and Regulation Skills

True healing also requires learning how to sit with uncomfortable emotions without fleeing into old habits—whether that be anger outbursts, withdrawal, control, or denial. Here, I often draw from Dialectical Behavior Therapy (DBT), teaching clients distress tolerance strategies such as grounding exercises, self-soothing, and the use of safe physical outlets. Emotion regulation skills help clients differentiate between what can be changed in the moment and what must be endured with compassion. This process strengthens their capacity to ride emotional waves without being capsized by them.

6. Creating New Patterns

Finally, therapy becomes a space for experimentation. Clients are encouraged to practice new ways of responding to familiar triggers—assertiveness instead of silence, curiosity instead of judgment, self-compassion instead of harsh criticism. Sometimes this means role-playing conversations, sometimes it means setting boundaries in real relationships, and often it means learning to ask for help rather than retreating into isolation. These new behaviors disrupt the cycle of emotional indigestion, allowing emotions to flow, be processed, and released, rather than stored and silenced.

7. Integration and Sustained Growth

Healing is not a linear process but a continuous practice. As a therapist, I remind clients that emotional health is cultivated through repetition and gentleness, not through sudden transformation. By weaving together mindfulness, reflection, reprocessing, literacy, regulation, and new behavioral experiments, clients learn to live with greater emotional clarity. They move from a place of suppression and dependency toward self-awareness, autonomy, and authentic connection.

In essence, therapy is about reintroducing clients to their own inner lives. Emotional indigestion is what happens when we swallow our truths without acknowledgment. Healing comes when clients learn to taste, name, and digest those truths—transforming discomfort into growth, and silence into voice.

Recognizing and Addressing Resistance and Unconscious Patterns

It is important to acknowledge that some emotional patterns are deeply ingrained and may operate unconsciously. Clients might resist exploring these patterns or feel overwhelmed by the prospect of change. As therapists, our role is to create a safe, non-judgmental space that fosters curiosity and compassion toward oneself. Gentle exploration, patience, and validation are essential in helping clients uncover and work through their emotional indigestion.

Long-Term Healing and Integration

Addressing emotional indigestion is not an overnight process; it involves ongoing self-reflection, emotional processing, and the development of healthier habits. The goal is to help clients move toward greater emotional flexibility—being able to experience feelings fully without becoming consumed or stuck. Over time, this leads to a more balanced internal environment, less reactive cycles, and a greater capacity to handle life's inevitable stresses with resilience and clarity.

Focus on Action & Empowerment

Unlocking Emotional Freedom: Action & Intention

This moment is an opportunity to solidify your insights and set a powerful course for your emotional liberation.

Empowerment Questions:

Considering your path, what essential truth about yourself or your capabilities have you recently uncovered or re-embraced?

To honor this insight, what specific, actionable commitment will you make to yourself, starting today?

Your Next Action:

Promise to Yourself: On a piece of paper or in a digital note, write a concise promise outlining how you'll nurture your emotional freedom. Date it, and set a reminder to revisit it in 1, 3, or 6 months.

Affirmation for Your Soul:

Breathe in this truth and repeat it with conviction: "I consciously choose freedom. I embrace healing. I embody wholeness."

Reflection Questions

What kind of person do I want to be outside of this relationship?

If I were to build a joyful life alone, what would it look like?

Exercise

Future Self Visualization: Close your eyes and picture yourself one year from now, whole and independent. Write down what you see: where you live, what you're doing, what brings you joy.

Affirmation Creation: Write one affirmation that starts with: "I am whole even without..." and repeat it daily.

Reflection self-Emotional assessment

- Introduction: Naming the Silent Struggle
    - Key Lesson I Learned

Recognize emotional indigestion and its impact on selfhood and health.

▪ Reflection Questions

Do I rely on others for my happiness or purpose?

Have I forgotten what joy feels like from within myself?

▪ My Small Step This Week

Recall 3 moments when you felt happy alone.

▪ My Affirmation

I was whole before; I can be whole again.

▪ Notes / Free Writing

▪ Who Am I Without My Partner?

▪ Key Lesson I Learned

Write 2–3 sentences about what stood out most to you.

▪ Reflection Questions

How would I describe myself without my roles in this relationship?
What dreams, hobbies, or interests have I neglected?

▪ My Small Step This Week

Revisit one hobby or interest for 15 minutes this week.

▪ My Affirmation

I am more than my roles; I am a whole person.

▪ Notes / Free Writing

▪ The Body Remembers

▪ Key Lesson I Learned

Write 2–3 sentences about what stood out most to you.

▪ Reflection Questions

How does my body react when I feel stressed in my relationship? What physical signs show that I am suppressing emotions?

▪ My Small Step This Week

Keep a daily log of body signals for one week.

▪ My Affirmation

My body speaks the truth, and I will listen.

■ Notes / Free Writing

▪ Women Trapped in Dependency

▪ Key Lesson I Learned

Write 2–3 sentences about what stood out most to you.

▪ Reflection Questions

What fears keep me in this relationship?

If I had resources and support, would I leave or stay?

▪ My Small Step This Week

Write one skill you have that could help you build independence.

▪ My Affirmation

I am capable of creating safety and stability for myself.

■ Notes / Free Writing

▪ Emotional Indigestion Beyond Poverty

▪ Key Lesson I Learned

Write 2–3 sentences about what stood out most to you.

▪ Reflection Questions

Am I staying for love or for lifestyle/status?

Which joys in my life are truly mine, independent of others?

▪ My Small Step This Week

Spend one day enjoying a simple pleasure (walk, music, cooking).

▪ My Affirmation

My value is not measured by lifestyle, but by my wholeness.

■ Notes / Free Writing

▪ Men and Emotional Indigestion

▪ Key Lesson I Learned

Write 2–3 sentences about what stood out most to you.

▪ Reflection Questions

What fears do I hide to appear "strong"?

Do I link my worth to my partner's presence or approval?

▪ My Small Step This Week

Share one honest fear with a trusted friend or write it privately.

▪ My Affirmation

True strength is found in honesty, not in silence.

■ Notes / Free Writing

▪ Therapists and Healers Are Not Exempt

▪ Key Lesson I Learned

Write 2–3 sentences about what stood out most to you.

▪ Reflection Questions

Do I give advice to others that I haven't applied to myself?

Where do I still carry unresolved emotional indigestion?

▪ My Small Step This Week

Practice one piece of advice you often give others this week on yourself.

▪ My Affirmation

I deserve the same healing I guide others toward.

■ **Notes / Free Writing**

▪ Communities in Pain

Key Lesson I Learned

Write 2–3 sentences about what stood out most to you.

▪ Reflection Questions

What beliefs about relationships did I inherit from family/community?

Do these beliefs help me or trap me?

▪ My Small Step This Week

Rewrite one inherited belief into a healthier alternative.

▪ My Affirmation

I can break cycles of pain and begin new patterns of freedom.

■ Notes / Free Writing

▪ The Fear of Going Back

▪ Key Lesson I Learned

Write 2–3 sentences about what stood out most to you.

▪ Reflection Questions

What is my biggest fear about leaving this relationship?
Is this fear based on reality or fear of judgment?

My Small Step This Week

List top 3 fears about leaving and brainstorm one step to reduce the smallest fear.

▪ My Affirmation

I am strong enough to face change and start over.

▪ Notes / Free Writing

▪ Healing Pathways

▪ Key Lesson I Learned

Write 2–3 sentences about what stood out most to you.

▪ Reflection Questions

What kind of healing feels natural to me (therapy, journaling, prayer, group support)?

What small act of independence can I try this week?

▪ My Small Step This Week

Do one daily act of self-reliance and journal how it feels.

▪ My Affirmation

Each small step I take leads me toward freedom.

▪ Notes / Free Writing

▪ Reclaiming the Self

▪ Key Lesson I Learned

Write 2–3 sentences about what stood out most to you.

▪ Reflection Questions

Who do I want to be outside of this relationship?

What kind of life would I love to build for myself?

▪ My Small Step This Week

Write a one-page vision of your future self, free and whole.

▪ My Affirmation

I am whole, complete, and free to create a new story.

■ **Notes / Free Writing**

▪ Conclusion: Towards Emotional Freedom

▪ Key Lesson I Learned

Write 2–3 sentences about what stood out most to you.

▪ Reflection Questions

What part of myself have I rediscovered in this journey?
What one commitment will I make to myself today?

▪ My Small Step This Week

Write a short promise to your future self and seal it for reflection later.

▪ My Affirmation

I choose freedom, healing, and wholeness.

Conclusion

In summary, emotional indigestion reflects a pattern of unresolved, recurring emotional responses that diminish well-being. As therapists, our work involves guiding clients to recognize these patterns, understand their origins, and develop healthier ways of engaging with their emotional experiences. Through mindfulness, reflection, emotional literacy, and coping skills, clients can begin to digest their emotions more effectively, leading to greater inner harmony and psychological health. Cultivating this awareness and skill set is an essential step toward lasting emotional resilience and personal growth.

◈ In what ways might I be avoiding or suppressing difficult feelings?

◈ Our culture often encourages us to "be strong" or "just get over it," leading many to unconsciously push uncomfortable emotions – like fear, shame, grief, or anger – deep down. Reflect on the subtle and not-so-subtle ways you might be doing this. Are you constantly busy?

◈ Do you distract yourself with food, entertainment, or substances?

◈ Do you intellectualize your feelings rather than truly feeling them?

◈ Recognizing these avoidance tactics is vital, as suppressed emotions rarely disappear; they often manifest as physical ailments, chronic stress, or unexplainable inner turmoil.

◈ How have my dependency behaviors affected my personal growth and relationships? This question calls for an honest self-assessment regarding any external crutches you might rely on – whether it's dependence on others for validation, on substances for comfort, on work for self-worth, or on specific routines for a sense of security.

◈ Explore how these dependencies might be hindering your ability to stand on your own two feet, make independent choices, and cultivate genuine self-reliance.

◈ Furthermore, consider the ripple effect on your relationships: Do these behaviors create imbalance, foster resentment, or prevent true intimacy and authentic connection?

◈ What steps can I take today to acknowledge and validate my emotional experiences? Moving from awareness to action, this question focuses on empowering you in the present moment.

◈ Acknowledging your emotions means granting them permission to exist without judgment, labeling them, and allowing yourself to feel them fully. Validating them means accepting that your feelings are legitimate given your experiences, even if others don't understand them.

◈ Consider practical steps: Could you do journal about your feelings?

◈ Talk to a trusted friend or therapist? Practice mindful breathing to sit with discomfort? Or simply offer yourself a moment of self-compassion when an emotion arises?

- How can my community support a culture of emotional honesty and healing? We don't heal in isolation. This question expands your focus beyond the individual, inviting you to consider the collective.

- Think about your family, friends, workplace, or spiritual community.

- What actions, conversations, or shared practices could foster an environment where it's safe to be vulnerable, express authentic feelings without fear of judgment, and collectively work towards emotional well-being?

- How can you contribute to building a space where empathy thrives and healing is a shared journey, not a solitary burden?

Engaging with these questions is more than an academic exercise; it's a profound act of self-love and courage. It lays the essential foundation for genuine self-awareness, allowing you to untangle complex emotional threads and understand the root causes of your behaviors. Ultimately, this deep dive empowers you to make conscious, deliberate choices that move you beyond old patterns and propel you towards true emotional freedom, authentic living, and a flourishing life.

Envisioning a Future of Whole and Healthy Communities

My deepest hope is for communities where individuals live whole, healthy, and free of silent suffering. Such communities foster environments where emotional expression is normalized, and seeking help is seen as a strength rather than a weakness.

When people confront their indigestions and choose healing, they not only transform their own lives but also contribute to a collective vibration of authenticity and resilience.

Imagine neighborhoods where vulnerability is embraced; workplaces where emotional well-being is prioritized; families where honesty and compassion flourish. Achieving this vision begins with each person willing to confront their inner indigestions, choose healing, and step into their authentic self.

Final Thoughts: Embrace the Journey

As a therapist committed to guiding others toward emotional freedom, I affirm that the journey from dependency to selfhood is profound and worthy. It requires facing discomfort, embracing vulnerability, and cultivating inner resilience.

The path may be challenging, but it leads to liberation—a life where you live whole, healthy, and free from silent suffering.

Confront your indigestions. Choose healing.

And become part of a movement towards communities where emotional health is a collective priority. The world needs your authentic self—brave, whole, and free.

Conclusion: Towards Emotional Freedom

Key Arguments

- Emotional indigestion is universal—cutting across class, gender, and culture.
- The way forward is through courage, self-recognition, and healing.
- A vision of communities where relationships are chosen freely, not lived as prisons of dependency.

Examples

- Revisit earlier stories with hopeful endings: from sickness to healing, from silence to voice.
- Closing call: "You were whole before, you can be whole again."

Reflection Questions

1. What part of myself have I rediscovered while reading this book?
2. What one step will I commit to for my emotional freedom?

Exercise

- Commitment Letter: Write a letter to your future self, promising one action you will take to heal from emotional indigestion. Seal it and read it after six months.

- Healing Journal

1. Key Lesson I Learned in This Chapter

- (Write 2–3 sentences about what stood out most to you.)

- My Reflection Questions

- What truth about myself did this chapter reveal?
- Where do I see emotional indigestion in my own life?
- What is one fear or barrier I need to acknowledge?

- (Space for reader to write answers)

3. My Small Step This Week

(Write down one practical, doable action inspired by this chapter. Keep it realistic and simple. Example: "Cook one meal for myself this week" or "Write in my journal every evening for 10 minutes.")

4. My Affirmation

(Rewrite a personal statement of strength. Example: "I am not defined by my relationship; I am whole on my own.")

5. Notes / Free Writing

(A blank section for the reader to capture emotions, fears, or memories stirred by the chapter.)

Did you love *Emotional Indigestion Illness Shaping Bodies, Families, and Communities*? Then you should read *The Healing We Never Spoke Of: Therapy*[1] by Branny Mthelebofu!

[2]

For professionals, the book acts as a guide for culturally informed therapy, drawing on the works of Freud, Jung, Ferenczi, and integrating film, art, and novel-writing as tools to engage patients creatively. It challenges therapists to listen with cultural humility and emotional curiosity, not clinical distance. What if your sadness isn't just yours—what if it's inherited silence? In the heart of South Africa's villages, and beyond, people carry unspoken burdens—grief that was never named, love that was never returned, questions that were never asked. This is not just a story about therapy—it is a journey into forgotten feelings, buried memories, and the cultural

1. https://books2read.com/u/mZDKx5

2. https://books2read.com/u/mZDKx5

silence that keeps so many from seeking help. It speaks to the widows who never cried, the men who confuse control for love, and the children who inherited pain before they learned to speak. Blending narrative storytelling, psychoanalysis, traditional wisdom, and prayer, this book is a bridge between the modern therapist's couch and the rural fire hearth. Whether you believe in dreams, ancestors, or dialogue—this book invites you to see healing not as betrayal of culture, but as a return to wholeness. Therapy is not introduced as a Western import, but as a tool that can be adapted to fit the language, rhythm, and values of village life.

Read more at https://www.facebook.com/branny.smithsa/.

About the Author

Dr Branny Mthelebofu is a multifaceted South African creative whose work bridges the realms of storytelling, healing, and music. As a public health specialist, filmmaker, nutrition therapist, holistic counsellor, and musician, he channels his diverse talents into narratives that explore the complexities of the human psyche and the pursuit of inner peace.

Under the pen name Branny Smith, Dr Mthelebofu crafts stories that delve into personal challenges, emotional trauma, and the transformative journey toward self-understanding. His literary works, such as The Professor's Descent, Desperation, and Chasing Where There is Love, My Wedding Contract Too, Her Lover is Gone, often feature protagonists grappling with internal conflicts and societal pressures, reflecting his deep interest in mental health and psychoanalysis. Beyond writing, Branny Smith employs his background in holistic therapy to assist clients in achieving emotional well-being through interactive counselling sessions. His approach integrates scriptwriting principles to facilitate character development and personal growth, offering a unique therapeutic experience that resonates with individuals seeking happiness and fulfillment.

As a musician, Branny Smith composes lyrics that address life's challenges, happiness, and the quest for peace of mind, utilizing music as a form of therapy for his audience. His passion for mental health and storytelling converges in his creative endeavors, making his work a compelling exploration of the human condition.

Through his multifaceted career, Dr Branny Mthelebofu continues to inspire and guide others on their journeys toward self-discovery and emotional resilience.

Read more at https://www.facebook.com/branny.smithsa/.

Banny Joma

All about Research

About the Publisher

The publisher produces films, sound tracks, music (different genres) and also publishes books.